Zion's New Name

Why the Christian Church is in Continuity with Biblical Israel

Andrew M. Sibley

Fastnet Publications

ISBN: 978-0-9562146-0-7

Published by:
Fastnet Publications
Mill Close
Colyton
Devon
EX24 6EU
England

Printed by Lightning Source

By the same author: *Restoring the Ethics of Creation*, Annomundi Books, (2006)

The cover photo is of the carving on the inside of the Arch of Titus on the Via Sacra in Rome, constructed following the fall of Jerusalem in AD 70. The title 'Zion's New Name' comes from *Isaiah 62: 1-2*.

Table of Contents

Preface

This book is written in a spirit of respectful dialogue in order to build understanding and unity in the Church over a controversial area of study, but also with the desire to interpret Scripture in the right theological context. The main desire to write came in response to developments in Christian Zionism that seemed to me to be moving away from the gospel of Christ, especially following John Hagee's book *In Defense of Israel*. Firstly, I wrote a review of Hagee's book that is currently on the Evangelical Alliance website *In Defence of the Messiah: A review of In Defense of Israel by John Hagee* (12/12/2007).[1] This book developed from that review. It is still quite short and a more detailed treatment will be attempted when I have time.

There are varied opinions on the question of the legitimacy of the modern State of Israel in the Church today, and I hope in this discussion to offer a bit more clarity. It is important to love the Jewish people, especially as they have suffered so much in history, and I hope to have avoided careless use of language. When Jews were suffering greatly during the rise of fascism, many Christians in Europe rightly went out of their way to help them. Some German Christians formed the Confessing Church, signed the *Barmen Declaration*, and opposed the brutality of Nazi Germany, some even paying with their own lives for their stand. In the same spirit of concern for the victims of violence and oppression, many Christians now feel duty bound to speak up for the Palestinians as well as Jews. Equally though, we should be critical of the violence by Palestinian authorities and militant groups, such as Hamas, against Jews, and instead work for peace, justice and reconciliation between both communities.

I would also urge those who might disagree with some of these things to check them out for themselves as use of labels

---

[1] [http://www.eauk.org/theology/key_papers/holy-land/]

has become very confused in this area. I want also to say as well that I do not subscribe to replacement theology, believing instead, as the subtitle suggests, that the Christian Church is in continuity with God's purposes that have been revealed through the blessings given to Abraham, Isaac, Jacob-Israel, Joseph, Ephraim and Judah. All Christians are therefore, I believe, New Zionists, a people looking forward to the return of Christ and the New Jerusalem; and this Messianic promise is offered to Jews as well. I believe therefore that the Christian Church is the natural home for all people, Jews, Israelites and Gentiles.

Acknowledgements

I would like to thank Dr Farid Abou-Rahme for encouraging me to write this book and for writing a Forward. It was already a concern upon my heart, but a shared desire gave the impetus to write. Thanks also to Farid and Ilham for their kind hospitality, and thanks to Dr Nabil Abou-Rahme who kindly reviewed an earlier draft and provided some useful feedback. Nabil also understands the relationship between Christianity and biblical Israel in terms of continuity. Thanks to Reverend Dr Stephen Sizer for encouragement and offering an additional Forward. Also thanks to Dr Stephen E. Jones of God's Kingdom Ministries for his books and teaching material. Although there may be points of disagreement, his writing has encouraged me to research the Old Testament in much greater depth than I previously have done, especially as it relates to Joseph's birthright and the question of the northern Israelite exiles. Other works that have provided important material include study notes from Paul Wilkinson on replacement theology, together with further works cited in the footnotes and bibliography. Mike Gascoigne has also provided advice on setting up a publishing title, and advice on formatting the book, as have Lightning Source, and thanks to my brother Timothy for advice on setting up a website.

Zion's New Name

Forward

Dr. Farid Abou-Rahme

Books and articles written about the very popular subject of Prophecy in relation to end times and Israel, can be broadly put under four categories:

1. Those authors who take some ideas from the Bible and run away with them, adding fiction and imagination, resulting in popular books and films. The problem here is that many accept such books as the authority on future events and start taking the teaching from them rather than the Bible.

2. Authors who base all their writing on ideas put forward by icons of the past without questioning or examining those ideas. The problem with this is that we put our trust in writings of fallible men, however good they are, when we should be basing all on the Bible. Writers here seem to pick and choose some Bible verses and end up with all sorts of conclusions and charts as well as saying that many parts of the New Testament do not apply to us today!

3. Authors who write for political reason who seem to pick up verses out of context to prove and promote an idea with political ulterior motives. Such writings should not be accepted as Bible based teaching.

4. Finally there are authors who spend time studying the Bible as a whole, interpreting Old Testament by the New Testament teaching, studying the actual historic facts and thus building together some consistent thoughts about the subject. They are looking to share their findings with others to encourage them to research the subject further. Such writers do so for no political or popularity gain.

Zion's New Name

I have known Andrew Sibley for a number of years as we share the same passion for making Biblical Creation known. His style of studying, researching and writing fit in with category 4 above and hence I heartily recommend his new book 'Zion's New Name'.

No two people can agree completely on a vast subject like this. But amongst the books I have read on this subject, Andrew's book stands out in clarity, objectivity and sincerity. It is up to the readers to look at the points raised and go back to the Bible and check them out before taking them on board. There is so much authoritative, brain washing material on this subject out there. It is good to have a book that encourages us to check the evidence objectively.

I do not hide the fact that I am one of those mentioned by Andrew in the book; born to Palestinian parents who were true Christian believers living in Palestine, the Holy Land where Christ was born and where He shed his precious blood for our salvation. When I was 4 years old we lost our home and all our possessions and were forced to flee to Lebanon as refugees. However, I thank God for my parents, those older generation giants of faith, who taught me in words and actions as I grew up that although what was done to us by the Zionists was completely wrong, we must follow the example of our Saviour the Lord Jesus who suffered more, but forgave those who crucified him. I have done that and my desire is that the Gospel message will reach all people whether Jews, Moslems, nominal Christians, atheists or people of any other belief and that many will accept Christ as their Lord and Saviour because He is the only way to heaven. Then they will be ready to face whatever happens at the end of times because, when you have Christ, nothing else matters.

Dr Farid Abou-Rahme   April 2009

Zion's New Name

Revd. Dr. Stephen Sizer

What is the relationship between Israel and the Church? In my own two books, *Christian Zionism: Road Map to Armageddon* (IVP 2004) and *Zion's Christian Soldiers: The Bible, Israel and the Church* (IVP 2007) I argue the case for biblical covenantalism as an alternative to replacement theology and dispensationalist Christian Zionism. Others who have similarly argued from a covenantal perspective include David Holwerda, Steve Motyer, O Palmer Robertson and Cornelius Vemena.

Such an approach recognises that through history God has only had one people in the world, those who share the faith of Abraham, Isaac and Jacob. Instead of separating Jews from Christians, God's desire is that Christians should work towards unity, both within the Church, and between Israelis and Palestinians, because of and through the atoning sacrifice of Jesus Christ. Instead of division, biblical covenantalism reaffirms that the Church is Israel, renewed and restored in Christ, but now extending to the Gentile nations as well. Christians should therefore work for peace, justice and reconciliation between Israelis and Palestinians.

With continued debate in the Church concerning the modern State of Israel, Andrew asks; who is Israel? He starts his research by examining the history of the Israelite nations through the Old Testament together with a careful study of the writings of the prophets in that historical setting. Andrew notes that Christian Zionism's appeal to Abraham's blessing is wrongly applied; Paul in Galatians asserted that it has come upon the Gentiles through Christ, and the blessings spoken over Joseph, Ephraim and Judah by Jacob-Israel are generally ignored. Joseph was given possession of Jacob-Israel's birthright; Ephraim too was to be identified with Abraham, Isaac and Israel, but his descendents were to extend across the earth. Judah's blessing was to bring forth the Messiah. The Old Testament records that the northern tribes of Israel, including

those of Joseph and Ephraim, were taken into exile by the Assyrians in 721BC and at face value did not return to the land. The prophets though asserted that the northern Israelites were not forgotten or replaced by God.

Andrew argues that Christian Zionism has wrongly applied the writings of the prophets, overlooking the proper theological and historical context. The prophets in fact present a consistent message; firstly that the exiled northern Israelites were to return under the promised Messiah. Secondly, that the northern ten tribes of Israel were to be reunited with Judah. Thirdly, that this return and reunion was to be under the new covenant. The prophets also promised that the reunited nation would extend beyond the borders of the Holy Land to bless the Gentile nations.

Andrew also argues, through a careful reading of the New Testament, that the apostles understood their mission in the context of this prophetic writing. The good news concerning Jesus was to go out to the exiled northern tribes, as well as to Jews and Gentiles, all being united together under Christ. Following this covenantal approach, Andrew argues that there is now unity and continuity between historical Israel, Judah and Gentile Christians within the Church.

But where does this leave the theology of Christian Zionism? From this study Andrew argues that it may be seen as a form of replacement theology, because it ignores the full history of the twelve tribes and the full promises of God to Israel, and seeks to replace true Israel, that is now identifiable as the Christian Church, with one part of Judaism. Forms of Christian Zionism also seek to divide the Church and Judaism along Gnostic lines, when instead God wishes to include the Jews within Christ. In effect it is seeking to hide God's full revelation of Christ to the remnant of Judah, but if God's purposes are to be fulfilled then the gospel must be made accessible to all Jews as well. Furthermore, Andrew argues that the final conversion of Jews to Christ is not dependent upon the existence of a separate State of Israel. Instead of supporting a nationalistic Jewish state in Palestine, Christian' support should be focussed on working for peace and a just settlement between Jews and Palestinians in the land.

Revd. Dr. Stephen Sizer

Zion's New Name

Chapter 1

Who is Israel?

The overall purpose of this book is to seek to build unity within the Church on the question of Israel through a careful study, and to question the development of erroneous theology. The questions that need to be asked first relates to the relationship between Christianity and the modern State of Israel. Does the State of Israel still have a purpose within God's plan today, or is the Christian Church the spiritual representation of Israel upon the earth? Questions such as these arise in terms of eschatology, (the end-times), how the Old Testament sacrificial legal requirements are to be interpreted within the Christian Church, and how the Law of Moses relates to the person of Jesus the Messiah. It also arises when we question the nature of Israel today in terms of political status, ethnic identity and in terms of legal claims and spiritual reality. There is though divided opinion within the evangelical community over this relationship, and also different opinion over how events will play out in the end-times. I want to stress from the start that this study is written on the understanding that God loves both Jews and Palestinians equally, and that the great commission of Jesus Christ is to preach the gospel throughout the earth, and thus make disciples of all people and nations within God's kingdom.

Through a study of Christian history two basic views can be identified and broadly categorised in regard to the place of Judaism and Israel in relation to the Christian Church. The first position is usually known as *replacement theology*, the second more recent view as *Christian Zionism*. These characterised positions though resemble a polarised type of argumentation, which has caused division in society in the past. In light of these different and opposing views that have arisen in Christian history, and brought to the fore in recent years, it is necessary to seek to find where the truth lies through a careful study of

Scripture. Scripture though needs to be interpreted within the correct context of its historical, social, spiritual and political setting in order to discover the intended meaning of the authors. The purpose here then is to ask; who is Israel? The Bible does in fact have a lot to say about the promises that God has made to Israel through biblical history. In examining these promises of God to Israel, it is not the intention here to deliberately engage in contentious theological disagreement for the sake of it, but to simply examine the Scriptures and to ask what they says about this subject so that a better understanding might be developed. However, this is a difficult subject because views are often strongly held, and each side believes they are committed to Christian orthodoxy. But there are legitimate questions relating to the danger for Christians of wrongful theology. One further concern that appears to me to be real, is that many Christian Zionists have placed such great faith in Israel that if something were to happen to the State of Israel that doesn't fit their eschatological scheme then their Christian faith would be severely shaken.

As noted, the debate also seems quite polarised with some supporters of Christian Zionism continuing to support the dispensationalism of J.N.Darby.[2] This theology was quite divisive when first proposed in the nineteenth century, being partly responsible for the split in the emerging Brethren movement. Other Christian supporters of Zionism further suggest that those opposed to Zionism in any form are anti-Semitic on the basis that the Jews have a right to their homeland and this should not be opposed at all; not even apparently on the basis of a reasoned theological argument which notes the conditional nature of God's promises regarding occupation of the land. This approach also confuses and conflates Israel as a political secular state with Judaism as a religious movement or identity. It is indeed possible and important to love Jews as a

---

[2] Wilkinson, P.R. *For Zion's Sake, Christian Zionism and the Role of John Nelson Darby*, London: Paternoster, 2007.

people, without necessarily supporting political, nationalistic Zionism, and being opposed to the latter doesn't have to collapse into anti-Semitism.

On the other side, even someone of the stature of Jimmy Carter has suggested that the Zionist policies of the State of Israel are in effect a form of apartheid because they seek to exclude Palestinians from the land.[3] The inference is that those Christian supporters of Israel, who then accept that Jews have pre-eminent rights over the land, are guilty of supporting apartheid policies by association. Each side then is effectively accusing the other side of racism by calling into question the beliefs of the other. It is to be hoped here though that a reasoned discussion can be had without using emotive language that doesn't really facilitate respectful dialogue. In this book I don't want to accuse Christians of racism because I don't think that is the intention of believers on either side. However, I will question whether it is right for Christians to support militant nationalism of any kind, whether Israeli or Palestinian, from a theological position. Christians are being caught up into a heavenly spiritual kingdom and thus called to make disciples of all nations bringing God's kingdom down to earth. Love and support for Palestinians and Jews as people and communities is central to the gospel and it is necessary to recognise that the issues are very important in terms of righteousness and justice for all.

This study stems from a personal quest to understand the issues, partly as a result of dissatisfaction with existing ideas on both sides of the debate, but also out of an understanding that a few passages in the Bible do seem to speak of the reappearance of the State of Israel in the last days, although equally many passages now attributed to the modern State of Israel have historically been interpreted in terms of the Church as being the spiritual manifestation of Israel.

---

[3] Carter, J, *Palestine: Peace not Apartheid*, New York, Simon and Schuster, 2006, reported in Sizer, S., *Zion's Christian Soldiers?* IVP, 2007, p. 15

Many Christians have also rightly hoped for, and prayed for the Jews, both through Christian history and in the present time, that they will come to see Jesus Christ as their own promised Messiah and risen King, and I would encourage this aspect of concern for Jews. Many Christians have also rightly rejected anti-Semitism and expressed concern for the suffering of Jews in history as well. For many years I personally accepted some of the moderate Christian Zionist arguments, perhaps similar to those espoused by David Pawson in his recent book *Defending Christian Zionism*,[4] and believed that God had a divine purpose for the nation of Israel in this present time in which the Jews were experiencing the biblically promised resettlement in their own land before our eyes. Afterwards, I believed, they will one day experience a national revival and therefore turn to their Messiah en-masse because their final conversion will mean life from the dead for all (*Rom. 11: 15*). However, this is the moderate view concerned with love for Jews as people. Other teachings of Christian Zionists have been developed that are of greater concern, which turn love for Jews into nationalistic support for the State of Israel, a state that is believed to be fulfilling God's purposes today. But in recent years an increasing number of Christians have become dissatisfied with this and believe that these views need to be questioned for various reasons, as characterised here.

Firstly, the violence brought to bear against Palestinians in recent years (many of whom are Christian, but now largely Muslim due to different rates of exile and birth rates), by the Israeli authorities cannot be overlooked by those committed to the teachings of Jesus Christ. Of course Palestinian terrorists have caused much suffering to the Israelis as well, through rockets and suicide bombings for instance, but it is only necessary to look at the death toll on each side to see which side

---

[4] Pawson, D., *Defending Christian Zionism*, Terra Nova Publ., 2008; See also Torrance, D.W., & Taylor, G., *Israel God's Servant*, London: Paternoster Press, 2007.

has the greater firepower and is causing the greater suffering. Of course some may argue that the Palestinian side often instigates the violence, which is true in part, although ultimately this is debatable. It was initially Zionist terrorism that sought to drive the British Mandate forces out of the land and forced Palestinians from their historical lands. Today Palestinians continue to lose their land with forced expulsions and many are living in a virtual concentration camp under siege conditions in Gaza with their human rights and liberty to travel denied. Any reading of the Gospels, or the Old Testament prophets such as Micah (*Mic. 6: 8*), shows that God has always required justice and mercy from his people the Israelites, even to the non-Jews who lived amongst them. In other words, it may be asked whether the current policies of the State of Israel are in fact in accord with the Mosaic Law let alone the loving teachings of Jesus Christ.

Some have suggested that inciting child suicide bombers against Jews is a form of child sacrifice, and inferring that because of this Palestinians are rightly being exiled from the lands.[5] In the Old Testament the Israelites were sometimes told to wipe out those people and nations who were engaged in idolatry with their practices of self-mutilation and child sacrifices, but that is hardly applicable to the Palestinians today, some of whom are Christians, or to the Muslims who claim allegiance to some of the Old Testament prophets through Islam. As far as I know Palestinian Muslims do not worship pagan gods such as Baal, Molech or Ishtar, but claim to worship the God of Abraham, who they identify as Allah[6], and many are opposed to militancy and suicide bombings even though they have not yet come to understand and accept the full knowledge of God as Father through the work of Jesus Christ and the indwelling Holy Spirit. I would suggest that some individual

---

[5] See bibliography.
[6] A further claim is that 'Allah' is really the pagan moon god. I have not studied this claim in depth and offer no further thoughts.

Muslims ought to be categorised in the same way as Cornelius who was said to be devout and God-fearing and diligent in doing good deeds and prayer (*Acts 10: 2*). However, even Cornelius was in need of salvation through Christ, as are Muslims. Other Muslims though preach violence and hatred and some Islamic institutions seem to be bordering on the demonic by encouraging children to hate Jews and non-Muslims and become suicide bombers. Inciting children to blow themselves up is indeed abhorrent and cowardly, but using this argument against all Palestinians is weak for a number of reasons. The Palestinians were being expelled before the suicide bombings started, and I would guess that most Palestinians do not support it. Further, it could be argued that the cause of the violence is a response to the brutalisation of the Palestinians by the authorities in the State of Israel.

Secondly, the history of Christianity in Palestine can be traced back to the time of Christ and the apostolic Church, and it has been a large Christian community that has been reduced severely since the creation of the State of Israel. The rights of the Christian community in Palestine need to be acknowledged and respected by Christians in the western nations. While many Christians in Palestine are of Arab descent there is a strong contingent of Levantines, the pre-Arab Christians, and some Maronites, whose presence as a community pre-dates the coming of the Arabs with the Islamic conquests. There is concern that unless a permanent peace settlement is reached between Israel and the Palestinians the Christian community might disappear altogether. A brief history of the Christian community in Palestine, and the scale of the decline, is discussed more fully in Appendix 2.

Thirdly, the State of Israel, as a nation, shows no outward sign of repentance and conversion to Christ despite existing as an independent state in the land for over sixty years. It may also be noted that repentance was a pre-requisite for resettlement in the land according to the Law of Moses, as exemplified by the way in which God brought Judah back from

Babylon. There are also very severe laws against the evangelism of Jews in Israel, and Messianic Jews are not really considered true Jews by the authorities. In other words, modern Israel is extremely resistant to the gospel of Jesus Christ and is often hostile to Palestinian Christians and also to Jewish Messianic believers. However, there are reports that some Jews are converting to Christ despite the restrictions, which is encouraging indeed.

Fourthly, the teachings of some leading Christian Zionists, as exemplified by John Hagee for instance, are questionable and arguably moving away from traditional Christian theology and the core positions of the Church. It is claimed for instance that Jews do not need to come to Christ because of a national 'election' following the covenant given to Abraham. This needs questioning in detail in light of the gospel. The American branch of the Lausanne Consultation on Jewish Evangelism has also recently pronounced in favour of spreading the gospel to Jewish people in its Resolution on Christian Zionism and Jewish Evangelism[7], calling on those who love and work amongst Jews to seek to bring the gospel to them.

Fifthly, some Zionist' positions require the formation and continuation of the State of Israel so that it may experience destruction through another holocaust in the final battle of Armageddon, after the Christian rapture. While most of us have little influence over political and military activity, some of those who do support Israel have enormous influence in American politics and use that influence to support their militant Christian theology. Whatever is to happen in the future, the Christian mandate is to make disciples of all nations, thus bringing peace and justice to all, not to seek the ultimate destruction of a Jewish state and their Muslim neighbours through war. In response to this a detailed examination of Scripture is important to determine exactly what the Bible says about Israel.

---

[7] 26th Annual meeting of the American branch of the LCJE, held at Phoenix, Arizona 2-4 March 2009. [http://www.lcje.net/statements/resolution.html]

Sixthly, the origin and nature of the Talmud, and Jesus' condemnation of the 'Tradition of the Elders' that was nullifying the authority of the writing of Moses and the Old Testament prophets is also relevant and ought to be questioned openly. The Talmud is considered to be more authoritative than the Torah, the five books of Moses, by many Jews today (although there are some Jews who reject the Talmud in favour of the Torah). Without going into detail, it may be noted that many in the State of Israel do not base religious authority upon the Law of Moses, but upon an interpretation of Moses that Jesus rejected. Many Christian Zionists are not aware of this distinction. This rejection of Moses is also born out in the symbolic six-pointed Star of David that is not an Old Testament symbol.

It is such observations that I believe call into question the true nature of the State of Israel in its standing before God, and it may be questioned how a largely secular, nationalistic Zionist movement can be fulfilling God's purposes today. Perhaps the Israelis will experience a great revival in our time, and that is to be hoped for and prayed for, but from a human perspective such a national revival doesn't look very likely at present. The purpose of the reappearance of a state called Israel in the present time then is not entirely clear and as noted above there are a number of unresolved theological issues that ought to be addressed openly in light of Scripture. Many Christians have accepted Israel as a legitimate Jewish state before God having lost sight of the Jewish origin and nature of Christianity and have perhaps not studied and understood the prophets and apostles in sufficient depth. Importantly, Old and New Testament biblical writers have commented widely on this subject, and it is necessary to weigh the evidence carefully and therefore avoid an incomplete understanding of Scripture. As a result of the misunderstanding of God's purposes in the world today Christians run the risk of being misled by wrong theology.

So, common questions that are being considered concern the promises that God has given to Israel, and how these promises are to be fulfilled in history and in the present time.

Zion's New Name

General comments from leading Christian Zionists suggest that there are age-old promises that are only now being fulfilled in our present day as a result of the restoration of the State of Israel in the last sixty years. Comments by some other Christian Zionists are perhaps more extreme and require a thoughtful response. Perhaps unwittingly, and with zeal for a Zionist state, they are downplaying the position of Christ and introducing new, highly questionable teaching into the Church. Some of this represents a new development in studies relating to the State of Israel and end-times prophecy although it was also present in the nineteenth century discussion, but at the very least this teaching should be examined in a proper theological manner.

So the purpose in the following chapters is to examine the teachings on both sides and to see how closely each line up with what the biblical writers actually believed and taught. Although the interpretation of biblical prophecy is not always easy, it is possible to begin to build towards a more consistent and coherent picture through careful study. It will therefore be questioned whether it is possible to reach a more complete, or better understanding of Scripture that is more coherent than current divided opinion allows. And it is also to be hoped that re-examining the theological issues will lead to an improved understanding between supporters of Christian Zionism and replacement theology.

It must also be remembered that Christians are called to love all people and nations, and that includes the Jews of the Diaspora, the Jews, Christians and Arabs of the State of Israel, and the Palestinians of the areas of the West Bank and in Gaza. However, that love can only be expressed within a context of honest dialogue, especially in light of the State of Israel's treatment of Palestinian people, many of whom are Christian; not forgetting also the terrorism and violence against the Jews by Palestinian extremists as well. Christians need to show Christ's love to both communities by working for peace, understanding and justice.

While it is true that many Christians hold to moderate theological views in this area, as noted each side also has its more extreme elements. Sadly, through history, Christian authorities have often failed to live up to Christ's commands to love even one's enemies, and have persecuted Jews down through the ages. Luther for instance initially embraced the Jews when it suited his rise to power, but once his position was secure he turned against them, perhaps through malicious negative reports by opponents of the Jews (although to be fair to Luther and the Reformation period it may be noted that there was also persecution against Calvinists and the Anabaptists; and Protestants and Catholics were being killed and executed across Europe for their faith during this time). Jews have though suffered much through the last two thousand years, often becoming exiles and wanderers throughout the world. In the last century Hitler too turned against the Jews and suggested that Luther would be with him, although Hitler, being an atheist or pantheist, was really no friend of Christianity either, claiming that he would abolish the established church having nationalised large sections of it under the banner of the German Church. Hitler's real beliefs are notoriously difficult to interpret, but his stated position was that of 'Positive Christianity,' which was really a materialistic belief system devoid of any real spiritual significance or reality.[8] Hitler tried to maintain some aspects of Christianity, but within a severely nationalistic and brutal context where Christianity was denied any real spiritual significance and meaning. Other German Christians of the Confessing Church, such as Karl Barth and Dietrich Bonhoeffer, signed the *Barmen Declaration* and in fact rejected Hitler's fascist state, some suffering persecution and death for their stand against extreme nationalism and support for Jews.

---

[8] Positivism, (sometimes known as scientism) is the assertion that only objectively verifiable statements can be accepted as true, although as this statement itself is not objectively verifiable, then the position is self-refuting.

Chapter 2

Replacement Theology

It is claimed by some Christian Zionists that through much of Christian history the Church has taught that it has superseded or replaced Judaism, and that by default this represents a persistent 'running sore' of anti-Semitism in the Church that needs to be addressed and eradicated.[9] This theology is sometimes known as *replacement theology,* or *supersessionism* in America, and *substitution theology* in parts of Europe. The New Testament has much to say on these matters (as will be discussed later), but after the New Testament period the early Church continued to try and fit the emerging Christian faith within an historical and global context as the Church was losing its initial Jewish identity.

The Church Fathers

Justin Martyr, who lived between AD 100-165, commented in *Dialogue with Trypho, a Jew* that the Church had become the true spiritual Israel through the crucified Christ. There was a tendency in Justin's writing to spiritualise the Old Testament, and he argued that in God's justice and fairness God was now punishing the Jews with exile from their historical lands for killing the prophets and the Messiah, but that God in his mercy and grace had spared them as a people.[10] Origen, in *Contra Celsus,* argued that the Jews couldn't be restored to God apart from Christ, because of the crime they had committed

---

[9] See for instance, Anglican Friends of Israel, 'Christian Aid adopts the Palestinian narrative and Replacement Theology', AFI website, 20th April 2009 [http://www.anglicanfriendsofisrael.com/content/view/75/33/]
[10] Justin Martyr, *Dialogue With Trypho* Chapter, 11and 16, in *Ante-Nicene Fathers: The Writings of the Fathers Down to A.D. 325* 1:200.

against Him.[11] Origen believed also that God has now divorced the Jewish nation and married the Gentile Church under the new covenant. Perhaps with some influence coming from the neo-Platonism of his time, Origen further spiritualised or allegorised the promises relating to Israel and applied them to the Church. There was a tendency then to allegorise Israel's blessings with application instead given to the Church, but to interpret punishments spoken against Israel as being literal. Cyprian of Carthage, a pupil of Tertullian who lived in the third century AD, also taught that the Jews had departed from God and thus lost God's favour, but subsequently Christians had 'succeeded in their place.'[12]

Augustine of Hippo argued that the Christian congregation was the true manifestation of Israel in the world commenting that; '...if [Christians] hold with a firm heart the grace of God which hath been given us, we are Israel.' And that 'The Christian people then is rather Israel.'[13] Augustine thought the Jews had become blind to their own Scriptures, but that in God's grace he had turned their offence into the 'salvation of the Gentiles.'[14] In *On Christian Doctrine,* Augustine argued that the Church has now possessed the Promised Land in a spiritual sense as spiritual Israel.[15] The early Church fathers were arguing that the Church was now the true manifestation of Israel on the earth because of the historical work of Christ, but largely in a spiritual sense.

It was though recognised that Gentile believers had been grafted into the Israelite olive tree, alongside the Jewish believers in Christ, during the earlier Christian period (*Rom. 11:*

---

[11] Origen, *Against Celsus* 4.22, in *Ante-Nicene Fathers: The Writings of the Fathers Down to A.D. 325* 4:506. Some references in this section are sourced via Paul Wilkinson's notes on replacement theology.
[12] Cyprian of Carthage in the Preface to *Three Books of Testimonies Against the Jews.*
[13] Augustine, *On the Psalms* 114.3 in *Nicene and Post Nicene Fathers* 8:550
[14] Augustine, *City of God*, Book XVIII Ch. 46.
[15] Augustine, *On Christian Doctrine*, Book 3: Ch. 34

11-24). However, as time progressed and the culture of Christianity became more and more Gentile in character and outlook, recognition of the Jewish origin and identity of Christianity was gradually lost. Instead of viewing the Church as an outgrowth from a Jewish root, the Gentile Church came to see that it had replaced Israel in God's plan. Replacement theology developed along non-scriptural lines and in later centuries was used to justify the maltreatment of Jews by Christian authorities.[16]

There was then a developing separation between Judaism and Christianity that was at least in part the work of the Church, but also in part due to the actions of the Jewish authorities who had persecuted the early Jewish Christian community, for instance by throwing James the half brother of Jesus off the roof of the temple and then stoning him to death. Christians also recalled that Stephen had been stoned to death as well, and this helped to deepen the sense of separateness and division between Jews and Christians. As a result of this division there was, I believe, a misinterpretation and misunderstanding of the full knowledge of Old Testament Scriptures by an increasingly Gentile Church.

Once the Roman Empire had legitimised the presence of Christianity, the Roman Catholic Church further worked to consolidate its power by enforcing acceptance of its central dogmas. With the conversion of the Roman Emperor Constantine to Christianity there was a desire to bring harmony to various theological disputes, and therefore the Council of Nicea was called to standardise theology and reject heresy, especially of the Arian variety. Thus the power of the western Gentile Church became increasingly centred in one place, that is

---

[16] It may be noted also that Judaism was developing away from its historical roots, with the Pharisaic Talmud becoming more and more authoritative in the lives of many Jewish people, over and above the Law of Moses, and the writings of the prophets. This may be seen as another form of replacement theology where the tradition of the elders was replacing the Law of Moses.

Rome, and the Jews were increasingly marginalized and separated from the Christian community. Eventually the Bishop of Rome came to take the place of the Emperor, and claimed jurisdiction across the whole of the known Christian world. With the Catholic Church exercising so much power, there were many opportunities for abuse, especially against the Jewish communities across Europe. The central dogmas of the Church were then imposed by force, which really ran against the teachings of Christ.

When Luther and the Protestant reformers challenged the authority of Rome, there was much bloodshed across Europe. Luther at first embraced the Jews, but when his own power was secure he turned against them (although he also turned against the non-conformist Anabaptists as well). Jews have subsequently suffered under Protestant and Catholic rulers. This is of course only a brief outline of Church history in relation to Jews, but a couple of points may be noted from this short historical sketch. Supporters of Christian Zionism make the claim that much of this antagonism against Jews is because of replacement-type theology. While I think that there is some truth in this claim the real causes run deeper, involving a struggle over Church authority and power, together with a lack of understanding and trust in both directions. But questions remain around the nature and adequacy of replacement theology.

Discussing Replacement Theology

R. Kendall Soulen has identified three views of supersessionism amongst Christian theologians.[17] Starting with the Church Fathers, Soulen comments that Origen and Hippolytus, and later Luther, argued for a *Punitive Supersessionism* where God has condemned, and is now punishing the rebellious Jews for rejecting Jesus as the promised

[17] R. K. Soulen, *The God of Israel and Christian Theology*, Minneapolis: Fortress, 1996.

Messiah. On the other hand Augustine and Justin Martyr focused on the practical purposes of God as *Economic Supersessionism*, where those who have accepted Christ have now replaced those Jews who rejected him. The third view is identified by Soulen as *Structural Supersessionism* where he notes that many Christians have rejected the Old Testament altogether considering it to be of much less importance to Christian conduct than the New Testament. Soulen notes that none of these views are mutually exclusive. From later discussions here it will become evident that the Old Testament has much to say about the current state of affairs and the idea of structural supersessionism is not entirely sustainable even though some aspects of the Mosaic Law relating to punishment have changed because of the work of Christ. What is of further interest is that some supporters of Christian Zionism seem to adopt aspects of supersessionism, particularly Soulen's punitive form. Pawson for instance, while arguing that the Jews are still a people before God, also comments that presently it is in a negative sense because they have been hardened.[18] There are dangers in arguing for a punitive type of replacement theology I believe, because it can easily descend into a call to persecute Jews as has happened in history (although Pawson is clearly not advocating this). But is God actively punishing rebellious Jews because they rejected Jesus? I will leave this question aside because of the difficulties it presents, but will comment that I would argue that according to Scripture the glory of the Lord, and his presence, have departed from old covenant Judaism and its system of worship, where Jesus commented to the Pharisees that their 'house will be been left to them desolate' (See *Matt. 23*). Pawson also seeks to categorise those who reject present day Zionism (he calls them anti Zionists) into supporters of liberal theology, replacement theology, fulfilment theology and

---

[18] Pawson, Op. cit., pp. 73-93

finally liberation theology.[19] However, he completely ignores those who believe the Church is a continuation of biblical Israel.

Another theologian, Novak, considers the 'new covenant' mentioned in Jeremiah *(Jer. 31: 31)*. He argues that there are basically three interpretive options. Firstly, that the new covenant is an extension of the old; secondly that it is an addition to the old covenant; or thirdly that it is a replacement of the old covenant. Novak notes further that in the New Testament the new covenant was considered either an addition to, or a replacement of, the old covenant.

Novak further argues from this that there are essentially two forms of replacement theology, which can be divided into a soft form and a hard form.[20] The soft form, he argues, considers the new covenant to be an addition to the old covenant, while the hard form considers it as a replacement to the old covenant. Novak comments that the soft form of supersessionism asserts that Jesus came to fulfil the old covenant promises, first for the God fearing Jews who accepted Jesus as the Messiah, then also for the Gentiles who accepted the covenant through him. There is then disagreement over those Jews who rejected Jesus; Novak comments that they should be seen as being under the old covenant because God's promises are irrevocable. Hard supersessionism on the other hand is the argument that the old covenant has been abolished once and for all, and Jews who continue to follow it are living in rebellion for rejecting Jesus. It will be pertinent to the following discussions to consider which of these views the New Testament writers asserted as being valid, (or if any are valid) but to some extent replacement theology has often been poorly characterised by supporters of Christian Zionism.

---

[19] Pawson, Op. cit., p. 15

[20] Novak, D., 'The Covenant in Rabbinic Thought,' in Eugene B. Korn (ed.), *Two Faiths, One Covenant?: Jewish and Christian Identity in the Presence of the Other*, Rowman & Littlefield, 2004, pp. 65-80.

However, an increasing number of Christians do not believe that replacement theology really captures the full purpose of God that is being worked out in the Christian Church and the world today. What I am arguing for in this book is that the new covenant is in fact the fulfilment of the continuing covenantal promise given to Abraham. From this it follows that the Christian Church should be identified as spiritual Israel, but also that it is legally, and also ethnically linked to descendants of both Judah and Israel; thus possessing both the birthright of Joseph's line, and being under the authority of the ruling Messianic king who was to come through David's line; that is Jesus Christ. In other words, I am arguing that Christians should accept the Jewish nature and origin of Christianity, and should identify more closely with the Jewish heritage of their faith as spiritual children of Abraham. For this reason I believe that it is correct to speak in terms of a Judeo-Christian continuity, because Christianity exists in unity and continuity with the remnant of the Judaic-Israeli nation, united with Gentiles in Christ. That is a remnant of Jews called out and reunited with the exiled Israelites and extending to the Gentiles according to God's promises in the Old Testament.

As for the Jews who rejected Jesus, Augustine thought that the persistence of the unbelieving Jews and the Old Testament Scriptures were both a testimony to the Church that was spreading throughout the nations. This, Augustine believed, provided evidence to the world that Christians had not merely made up their faith concerning Christ, but that it was attested to by Jewish history and prophecy.[21] A long and noble heritage was important for a faith system in those times and the continuation of Jews as a people was considered advantageous, especially as the Christian Church was becoming more influential across the known whole world. Augustine thought that although God had dispersed the Jews, he had not destroyed

---

[21] Augustine, *The City of God*, XVIII Ch.46. in *Nicene and Post Nicene Fathers* 2:389

them as an entire nation, but allowed them to exist as a separate group and therefore they were a testimony for Christians in the world. A number of scholars have noted that Augustine's comments had important social ramifications for the Jews, as Christians permitted Jews to continue to live amongst them because of their apologetic value as a testimony to the truth of Christianity.[22] The Roman Catholic Church continues to largely accept the testimony of the Church Fathers, although blended with a tendency to believe that it has replaced Israel, as does some sections of Protestant Christianity, although recently the Pope has had some dialogue with Jewish religious leaders to discuss differences.

Calvin's Covenantal Theology

The covenant theology of Calvin is also identified by some Christian Zionists as being a form of replacement theology, and thus a betrayal of the Jews. Wilkinson for instance comments that the 'adversus Judaeus' (against the Jews) tradition is enshrined in Origen and Augustine's allegorical theology, and that this is central to the reformed covenant theology of the *Westminster Confession of Faith* of 1646. Calvin was also influenced by the theology of Augustine, which shaped his view of the Church and Israel, even though he came to reject the authority of Rome.

Wilkinson calls covenant theology a 'philosophical system' that teaches that God has only ever had one people, this under an overarching covenant of grace that embrace all the biblical covenants.[23] There are, I believe, some important

---

[22] See for instance: Cohen, J., 'Introduction', in Jeremy Cohen (ed.), *Essential Papers on Judaism and Christianity in Conflict: From Late Antiquity to the Reformation*, New York: New York University Press, 1991, pp. 13–14 ; or Hood, J.Y. B., *Aquinas and the Jews*, (Philadelphia: University of Pennsylvania Press, (1995), p. 12f ; or Carroll, J., *Constantine's Sword: The Church and the Jews*, Boston: Houghton Mifflin, 2001
[23] Wilkinson, Op. cit., pp. 42-43.

differences between replacement theology and covenant theology. However, identifying the Church as a continuation of God's plan regarding Israel is not an argument that is against the Jews, but one that is in continuity and unity with the Jews. Neither is it fair to call it a 'philosophical system' as it is clearly a well-developed theological system, and I believe in fact formed the basis for Darby's dispensationalism.

Calvin for instance quotes from Matthew (*Matt. 8: 11*) and notes that Jesus Christ promised his followers that the only kingdom of heaven is one in which Christians may sit down with Abraham, and Isaac and Jacob,[24] and Calvin, like Luther, believed that Paul's use of 'Israel' in Romans (*Rom. 11: 25-26*) refers to the union between Gentile and Jewish believers.[25] Calvin believed then that the true Church (Gk. *Ekklesia*) existed amongst the Jews and Israelites in the Old Testament,[26] just as it did in the New Testament, but that the Church under the old covenant was in the form of childhood, compared to the coming-of-age of adulthood that was enabled by the new covenant.[27] The Law was thus appropriate for the old covenant, with the gospel of grace necessary for maturity.[28] Calvin noted that the prophets looked forward to the restoration of the Church of Israel according to the everlasting covenant that God had promised to David.[29] The overarching covenant was with Abraham, but that the outworking was in different modes of 'dispensations.'[30] Use of this word by Calvin suggests that

---

[24] Calvin, J., *Institute of the Christian Religion*. (IV.XVI.14) (Garland, TX Galexie Software, 1999. Quoted in Sizer, S., *Christian Zionism: Road Map to Armageddon,* IVP, 2004, p. 27

[25] Sizer, S., Op. cit., p. 27.

[26] Calvin, J., *Institutes of the Christian Religion*, (IV.II.7)

[27] Interestingly, the Septuagint (LXX) uses the Greek word Ekklesia to refer to Israel as the people of God in the Old Testament. Ekklesia is used for the church subsequently. See for instance Ladd, G.E., *The Gospel of the Kingdom*, Grand Rapids, Eerdmans Pulb., 1959, pp. 112-114

[28] Calvin, *Institutes*, (II.XI.2)

[29] Calvin, *Institutes*, (II.VI.4)

[30] Calvin, *Institutes*, (II.X.2)

Darby's dispensationalism is in reality an outgrowth and arguably a corruption of Calvin's covenant theology. But instead of the unity between the Church and Israel that Calvin had taught, there was instead division under a dual covenant system. As noted, Calvin also influenced the *Westminster Confession of Faith* of 1643. Chapter VII *Of God's Covenant with Man* for instance also states that the same covenant of grace has operated through history under various 'dispensations.' Chapter XIX *Of the Law of God* comments that God gave to the '…people of Israel, as a church under age, ceremonial laws…now abrogated, under the New Testament.'

In summary then, replacement theology does not adequately describe God's purposes in the world through his Church, which should, I believe, be viewed as a continuation and fulfilment of Israel's promises, not its replacement. However, replacement theology as commonly understood today is a poor characterisation of Christian theology as developed through history. Furthermore, Calvin's covenant theology forms the basis for a correct understanding of God's purposes in the world today. While there is truth in the claim that some theologians taught a form of replacement theology, this was not universal and there was a great deal of tolerance shown towards Jewish exiles in many periods. Undoubtedly though, there have also been periods of persecution which is deeply regrettable. The next chapter will look in more detail at the theology of dispensationalism and the rise of Christian Zionism.

Chapter 3

The Development of Christian Zionism

The other view that is common today is the belief that God still has a purpose for the Jews, and a Jewish state, in the last days outside of the Christian Church; this demonstrated, it is claimed, by the formation of the modern State of Israel on the 14th May 1948. Moves to restore the Jewish State of Israel began in the early nineteenth century, as evidenced for instance by the establishment of a British Consulate in Jerusalem in 1838. A group from the Church of Scotland also wrote a report, published in 1840, entitled a '*Memorandum to Protestant Monarchs of Europe for the restoration of the Jews to Palestine*' arguing for the re-establishment of a State of Israel.

One of the main theological influences for this interest in a new State of Israel came through Edward Irving and Henry Drummond who were instrumental in forming the Catholic Apostolic Church. Also influential was the Plymouth Brethren leader, and former Church of Ireland Minister John Nelson Darby. Darby later adopted and developed the pro-Israel theological framework of dispensationalism from Irving and Drummond's Zionist foundations. Darby it would seem was developing his dispensationalist theology through the 1830s and early 1840s with influence coming from both Irving and Drummond, although the origin of the theology of Christian Zionism and dispensationalism is often wrongly attributed primarily to Darby and therefore misunderstood. The origin of this emerging theology appears to stretch further back in time; Wilkinson for instance argues that various puritans believed that Jews would be restored to the land in the last days.[31] It is therefore important to look at the influences that led to the development of dispensationalism and Christian Zionism as

---

[31] Wilkinson, Op. cit. pp. 135-161

theological concepts afresh to see if it is possible to understand their origin a little better.

Promoting Christianity Among the Jews

Some of those who promoted the idea of the restoration of a Jewish state were involved with the London Society for Promoting Christianity Among the Jews (LSPCJ). The LSPCJ was formed in on the 4th August 1808 under the leadership of Joseph Frey, the son of a German Rabbi, with the original grand title of 'London Society for the Purpose of Visiting and Relieving the Sick and Distressed and Instructing the Ignorant especially such as are of the Jewish Nation.' On the 1st of March 1809 it was changed to the slightly easier LSPCJ, and within a few years had attracted some very notable supporters and patrons from leading society, and the evangelical community. In 1815 it was taken over by the Anglican Church as a result of debts and mounting costs of administration. Officially it did not take a view on the correct interpretation of eschatology, writing a disclaimer to that effect on the 27th October 1823 although many supporters believed in the physical restoration of the Jews to the land of Israel. As a result of the disclaimer the Vice President Lewis Way resigned because of his commitment to the return of Jews to the land before conversion to Christ.[32] Therefore it would appear that although many of those interested in the return of the Jews to the land of Palestine were involved with the LSPCJ, the organisation as a whole did not take a clear stand in that direction in the early nineteenth century. However, as Wilkinson notes, the 1881/2 Russian pogroms led the LSPCJ to issue a statement that they believed that this was part of a move of God to bring Jews back into their ancient lands.[33]

---

[32] Wilkinson, Op. cit., pp. 167-169.
[33] Wilkinson, Op. cit., p. 169.

Edward Irving

The Scottish Presbyterian Edward Irving was partly influenced by a number of Jesuit theologians having translated into English the work of the Chilean Jesuit Manuel de Lacunza, entitled *The Coming of Messiah into Glory and Majesty*, in a two-volume edition published in 1826 and 1827. Lacunza, who died in 1801, wrote in 1790 under the pseudonym of Ben Ezra, a supposed converted Jew. Although Lacunza rejected the historicist view of eschatology in favour of a futurist interpretation, he considered that the antichrist would be a person, or confederacy of people opposed to God and believed that the antichrist would be defeated before and during the period of the return of Christ. Lacunza did not teach the pre-tribulation rapture envisaged by Irving and Darby, although he did believe that Christians would be caught up into the air with Christ at the final conflagration and return with him to the earth in the 'day of the Lord's coming,' a 'day' that was thought to last for up to 45 earth days.[34] However, Lacunza in his eschatological scheme had believers returning to the earth during that 45-day period as messengers sent from God.[35]

The Jesuits had previously discussed both futurist and historicist views of the end times. The sixteenth century Jesuit Riberia had supported futurist eschatology where the antichrist would come and build a new temple in Jerusalem and outlaw Christianity, while the Jesuit Cuninghame, writing in 1813, believed Christ would return before the millennium reign mentioned in *Revelation*. On the other hand Alcazar, who died in 1613, and his followers, interpreted *Revelation* in terms of fulfilment through the first century Roman Empire. So, although Irving found some influence in Jesuit theology, this influence is far from the complete picture. As part of his translation of

---

[34] Lacunza, M. *The Coming of Messiah into Glory and Majesty*, (Trans. Irving, E.), (2 Vols.), Vol. II, 1826/27, p. 250.
[35] Lacunza, Op. cit., pp. 262-263.

Lacunza's work, Irving also wrote a 126 page 'Preliminary Discourse' for these volumes in which he set out his own views on the end times and support for a new State of Israel. Incidentally, this preliminary discourse was dated as being written during Christmas 1826, and it may be noted that Irving reached different conclusions to those drawn by Lacunza.

In 1826 Irving freely spoke in terms of dispensations and argued that the wickedness of the Gentile nations was such that God would bring judgement upon them and remove them from their place with only the elect saved and raptured into heaven (Irving quoted from *Isaiah 24* and applied it to the Gentiles).[36] Secondly, Irving argued, once God had judged the Gentiles for their unfaithfulness, God would restore a remnant of Jews, commenting that "The restoration of the Jewish nation, to be again the Church of God, and their re-establishment in their own land, to be the head of the nations, and the centre of the earth's unity."[37]

Another theme of Irving's theology was the restoration of spiritual gifts to the Church prior to the second coming, and there was some excitement at the house of James and George MacDonald, and sister Margaret, in Port Glasgow where manifestations of the Spirit were believed to be taking place. In March or April of 1830 Margaret believed she had a vision of a rapture where 'Spirit filled' Christians would be taken up into Christ before the antichrist was to be revealed, while the rest would go through the tribulation. This greatly impacted on Irving's beliefs, although a careful reading of the vision, if accepted as a valid prophecy, would suggest it should be read to mean that Spirit filled Christians would be protected through the tribulation that was to come, and that it was not speaking of a physical rapture prior to the second coming of Christ. She related the spiritual coming to the parable of the wise virgins

---

[36] Irving, E. 'Preliminary Discourse,' in Lacunza, M. *The Coming of Messiah into Glory and Majesty*, (Trans. Irving, E.), (2 Vols.), Vol. I, 1826, p. iv.
[37] Irving, E., Preliminary Discourse, Op.cit., pp. iv & viii.

who kept their lamps burning so that we '...may discern that which cometh not with observation to the natural eye.'[38] What is interesting about the vision of Margaret MacDonald is that it warns of a false-Christ to come who will test the true Spirit filled believers who are to go through the tribulation, and not be raptured out of it. Only those filled with the Holy Spirit would have the enlightened discernment once they had been brought into Christ afresh through a 'spiritual renewal' and thus they would be able to recognise the antichrist through the time of tribulation. She commented that there '...will be outward trial, ...but [it is] principally temptation.' And the 'trial of the Church is from Antichrist. It is by being filled with the Spirit that we shall be kept.'[39] Incidentally similar prophetic promises were given in the New Testament period to encourage the believers to persevere through suffering and deception. In this sense then the great tribulation should not be seen as simply a time of physical suffering, but a time also of testing and deception in the Church; and this has been the nature of threats to Christianity through history, with danger coming from external violence and internal false teaching. In the prophecy she further warns that some people were 'turning from Jesus' thus 'not entering in by the door', but 'passing the cross.'[40]

While it is possible then to read Margaret MacDonald's prophecy in terms of the ongoing work of the Holy Spirit in the present Christian age, others read it to imply that there would be a secret *physical* rapture to come that would mark a new dispensation for Jews apart from the Gentile Church. Drummond and Irving's quarterly journal, *The Morning Watch*, (also known as *The Quarterly Journal of Prophecy and Theological Review*) published a commentary under a pseudonym 'Fidus,' which argued in the September 1830 edition

---

[38] In Norton, R., *Memoirs of James and George Macdonald of Port-Glasgow*, 1840, pp. 171-176. Based on her hand written account of 1830.
[39] Ibid.
[40] Ibid.

that there would be a partial pre-tribulation rapture. In the June 1831 edition of *The Morning Watch* Irving made his own pre-tribulation teaching more explicit. Interestingly then it may be seem that Margaret's words had the same effect as some of Jesus' parables in that it blinded some eyes while opening the eyes of others (*Matt. 13: 10-17*).

According to Irving Jerusalem was to be established as the centre of God's plan for the re-emergent Jewish nation, and the world. Jesus was to come back, not in power and glory at first, but to take the Gentile saints away in a secret rapture where believers, both the dead and those still living, would be caught up to meet him in the air, therefore allowing people to escape the great tribulation that was to come upon the earth.[41]

As noted, Edward Irving, as well as being influenced by the Jesuits, was also closely associated with Henry Drummond, a descendent of an aristocratic Scottish banking family with Hungarian ancestry and also with links to well known Jewish banking families in Europe. Both Drummond and Irving helped to establish the Catholic Apostolic Church through a number of conferences on prophecy held in 1826 and 1830 in Drummond's stately home at Albury, Surrey. Drummond was closely associated with the LSPCJ, as was the prominent Joseph Wolff who was also present at the Albury meetings. Wolff was also of European origin and a Christian convert from Judaism who later named his own son after Henry Drummond. Drummond also wrote articles for *The Morning Watch* that he controlled with Irving and a few others. This journal often discussed ideas along the lines of dispensationalism and support for a new Jewish state, as well as discussions on such things as cabalism and reports of the various utterances from Christian prophetesses as noted above. Henry Drummond for instance had a letter published in *The Morning Watch* of the 1st September 1829 in which he enclosed a Jewish prophecy from a learned Rabbi by the name of Rabbi Samson of Oster Poli, who he described as a

---

[41] See for instance, MacPherson, D., *The Real Manuel Lacunza,* (nd).

'great Cabalist' and placed great credence on the word of this Rabbi who foretold judgement on France, Spain and Russia followed by the calling of the Jews and the coming of 'David.' Drummond further criticised the amount of effort the Church used in preaching the gospel, considered the '...bustle for the circulation of Bibles and Tracts, sending out missionaries, and emancipating the oppressed of mankind' to be a '...tremendous delusion.'[42] Instead Drummond believed that the Church should be primarily engaged in supporting the national restoration of Jews to their ancestral lands, and that this should be a central doctrine.[43]

There was great expectation and enthusiasm that God was doing a new thing through subsequent meetings of the Catholic Apostolic Church, but another developing stream that was to become known as the Plymouth Brethren was also shaped partly by conferences held at Powerscourt in Ireland between the years 1831 to 1834, although it should be noted that Brethren assemblies were developing prior to these conferences through the work of a number of travelling preachers such as George Muller, Henry Craik and Benjamin Wills Newton, especially in the southwest of England. A number of small Brethren assemblies were also developing in Dublin during the late 1820s with members including the Catholic Edward Cronin, Church of Ireland Minister J.N. Darby, Edward Wilson of the Bible Society and the Brethren missionary pioneer Anthony Norris Groves, amongst others.[44]

---

[42] Drummond, H., *Dialogues on Prophecy*, Vol I, London: James Nisbet, 1827, pp. 6, vi-vii; in Wilkinson, Op. cit., pp. 179-180.
[43] Drummond, H., *Dialogues on Prophecy,* Vol. I., p. 100; and Drummond, H., *Tracts for the Last Days*, Vol I, 1844, p. 344; in Wilkinson, Op. cit., p. 179.
[44] See Wilkinson, Op. cit., p. 76.

John Nelson Darby

Darby first came into contact with the idea of a national conversion and return of the Jews to Israel through Richard Graves, his tutor at Dublin's Trinity College. Darby studied theology and the classics at Trinity College, and later acknowledged that Graves had been an influence on him. Graves was notably involved with the Dublin branch of the LSPCJ and as early as 1811 was interested in the return of the Jews to the land, as was another of Darby's tutors, Richard Elrington.[45] According to Wilkinson, Darby was probably also influenced by some of the prophetic millennial writing and teaching of the Irish Catholics who he came into contact with in Ireland, such as the works of Charles Walmesley and Barney McHaighery.[46]

Darby was at first interested in converting Roman Catholics through preaching along with other like minded Protestants, and with some success with 600 to 800 conversions claimed per week across Ireland, but he became disillusioned by the actions of the Church of Ireland's Archbishop Magee, who wanted Catholic converts to recognise the supremacy of the Protestant faith and give their allegiance to the British Crown. A petition was organised and submitted to the British Parliament by the Church of Ireland authorities on the 1st February 1827 that sought protection against Rome, but it only put back the work of the Church with entrenchment on both sides and as a result the flow of Catholic converts dried up. This led Darby to reject political activism in the Church on the basis that God's kingdom was heavenly not earthly, likening the action of the Church of Ireland authorities to the Roman Church's authority they were opposed to.[47] This action by the Church of Ireland was perhaps a major catalyst that led him to fellowship in newly

---

[45] Wilkinson, Op. cit., pp. 73-75.
[46] Wilkinson, Op. cit., p. 72.
[47] Wilkinson, Op. cit., pp. 75-76.

formed assemblies in Dublin that were to form the basis for the Brethren movement and thus breaking with clerical authority. There is though some irony that while Darby wanted Christian faith to be free from political influence and non-conformist as part of a heavenly kingdom, his teachings helped to enable the formation of Christian and political Zionism, this on the basis that a national, political, earthly State of Israel was sanctioned by God, once the Church had been removed at the rapture.

At the Powerscourt conferences Darby was influential and the theology of dispensationalism was later to become more important to Darby than the apparent exercise of charismatic gifts that were becoming evident in Catholic Apostolic Churches. Benjamin Wills Newton, the Oxford Secretary for the LSPCJ chose not to attend the 12th annual meeting of that organisation, but instead decided to attend the Powerscourt meetings. Incidentally, other members listed in the 1827 annual report of the Irish branch of the LSPCJ included Lady Powerscourt as a patroness.[48]

In 1829 Darby was still apparently arguing in favour of a historicist view of prophecy with prophecies relating to Israel considered fulfilled within the Christian Church,[49] although Darby did address the 11th annual meeting of LSPCJ meeting in Plymouth in October 1830, but it wasn't until later in the 1830s that Darby fully accepted and developed the theology of dispensationalism. The second Powerscourt meeting in September 1832 further discussed the question of the status of a Jewish nation before God, and Darby wrote to the editor of the *Christian Herald* on the 15th October 1832 commenting that the delegates at the conference were concerned with questions such as 'by what covenant did the Jews, and shall the Jews, hold the land [of Israel]?'[50]

---

[48] Wilkinson, Op. cit., pp. 80-81.

[49] Darby, J.N., 'Reflections' *The Prophetic Inquiry,* No.1 1829, pp. 1-31

[50] In Wilkinson, Op. cit., p. 81.

Darby denied that Irving influenced him in his dispensationalist theology and it is likely that a number of factors were responsible for his change of mind during the 1830s, but some influence must have come through Irving and Drummond's publication *The Morning Watch*.

This quarterly journal sprang out of the Albury conference of 1828 and was financed by Henry Drummond with John Tudor acting as editor. It was to last for only four years.[51] Later, under the influence of the increasingly independent minded Irving, the Catholic Apostolic Church began praying earnestly for revival and an outpouring of the Holy Spirit, with claims for utterances of tongues at his Regent Square Church occurring in London in 1831. This perhaps did not fit well with those who had a stronger interest in the Jewish cause, and the accident-prone Irving died at the young age of 42. Walker comments that the writing of Drummond (and perhaps others) in this journal was a more likely source of Darby's developing dispensationalism through the 1830s,[52] although it is questionable from Darby's outward character how much credence he would (or should) have paid to prophetic utterances from cabalists. Darby had visited the MacDonald's house in 1830 to inquire about Margaret's prophecy, although he didn't seem too impressed with the words of prophecy from Margaret. Having said that it is also odd why Darby would have continued reading the journal that was apparently flirting with cabalism, when Darby was seemingly leading his Church grouping into greater outward purity and exclusivity, although it would seem that Darby was captivated by an interest in the new ideas relating to a Jewish nation that were being presented and discussed in that journal.

---

[51] Wilkinson, Op. cit., pp. 197-199.

[52] See for instance: Walker, A, *Restoring the Kingdom*, London: Hodder and Stoughton, 1985, pp. 218-222. Walker relies on a work by Rowdon, H. *The Origins of the Brethren*, Pickering and Inglis, 1967

Darby's Theology

The dispensationalism that Darby adopted and developed is, at its most simple, a division of history into periods of divine grace whereby God deals with people through covenants that he puts in place. In that sense it may be seen as an extension of Calvin's covenant theology. Under Calvin's scheme Christ's work of grace upon the cross was the means of salvation for all who lived before and after the cross, taking the Scripture that says that Christ was crucified from before the foundation of the earth. To Calvin, the cross was considered central to history, but Calvin believed that God has only ever had one lineage of people, one congregation upon the earth, a line that passed down from Adam to Noah, to Abraham to Isaac, to the Israelites before the tabernacle in the wilderness, to the remnant of Jews who came back from Babylon, and finally to the Church.

If that were all there was to the emerging theology of dispensationalism it would only be as controversial as Calvin's developed theology, but Darby, following Irving and Drummond, primarily associated dispensations of grace with a particular form of eschatology involving a pre-tribulation, perhaps secret rapture for the Gentiles together with the restoration of the Jews to the land of Israel where Jews may again approach God through the old covenant originally given to the Israelites at Mount Sinai. In other words, Darby's scheme offered a separate dispensation of grace to Jews from that given to Gentiles. In the form that Darby envisaged, the theology of dispensationalism is then associated with belief that God would restore the old covenant practices of worship, and if taken to its logical conclusion it also involves the rebuilding of the temple in Jerusalem following, or perhaps prior to, the secret rapture. In this scenario there is considered to be a spiritual dispensation of grace for Gentiles under the new covenant, but that there will be another earthly dispensation of grace under the old covenant that will be re-established in the end times. However, this theology in effect develops a false dualism between Israel and Christ; in effect placing division between the birthright that belongs to Israel (through Joseph and Ephraim) and the promised Messianic Judean ruler who was to rule over all the tribes of Israel. It divides then Israel from the Messiah, and it also divides Jews from Gentiles. However, as will be shown in later chapters, the prophets were emphatic that the promised Messiah was to come for Israel and Judah as well as the Gentile converts, thus bringing all things together, under one head.

Wilkinson though seeks to clarify exactly what Darby's theology entailed, although he notes that Darby has suffered from misunderstandings, partly because he is so difficult to read. What I think is also the case is that Darby was developing his theology throughout his life, and some of his earlier thoughts may not be consistent with later thinking. Wilkinson though firstly notes that Darby saw the Christian Church and Israel as two separate and distinct groups of people. Darby for instance, preaching from *Romans 9-11*, urged Christians to recognise that they have been grafted into the Jewish olive root, but Darby did not believe it necessary for Jews to be re-grafted onto their own root because he believed their initial calling as a nation was irrevocable.[53] For Darby, Israel had a national irrevocable calling, but Christianity was a gathering of saints.[54] In fact Darby further distinguished between the Church, the Gentile nations and Israel.[55] Darby believed that the Church, consisting of Jewish and Gentile believers, exists because of a spiritual dispensation, or parenthesis, with God's timeframe as it relates to Israel suspended until the rapture, therefore the Church is receiving heavenly promises and will be caught up with Christ into a heavenly place at the rapture. The Christian believers will govern the earth with Christ in heaven during the period of the

---

[53] Darby, *Romans*, 'Synopsis of the Books of The Bible,' Vol. 4, pp. 222-223; in Wilkinson, Op. cit., p. 97.
[54] Darby, *The Claims of the Church of Eng*land, 'The Collect Writings of J.N. Darby', Vol. 14, (1870) p. 197; in Wilkinson, Op. cit., p.102
[55] Wilkinson, Op. cit., pp.98-99

millennium. However, Israel's calling was national and earthly, and would form the seat for Christ's earthly rule. Christians then were considered by Darby to be in union with Christ having superior promises to those of Israel, but Israel belongs to God as an earthly nation.[56] This does though have the appearances of the type of Gnosticism that the apostles taught against being derived from forms of Greek philosophy. Such pagan philosophy, especially that of neo-Platonism, tended to divide the material from the spiritual, and it led to a dualism that was often characteristic of Gnostic teachings. Darby's system then falsely separates 'earthly' Jews from the 'spiritual' Church and the Messiah, in effect denying God's full revelation of Christ to Jews.

According to Darby, during the seven-year period of the tribulation many of the events of *Revelation* would take place with a struggle between the Jews and Satan for their souls with the Jews for a time siding with the antichrist, and in the end only a remnant of Jews will be saved when Christ comes back to his earthly throne at the end of the great tribulation period. Although Darby believed in a national salvation for Israel outside of the Church, only a remnant would be left alive at the end of the great tribulation. Many Christian Zionists generally fail to see the sad irony in this theology, in that while they claim to love Jews, in reality it involves the destruction of a majority of re-gathered Jews in another holocaust.

Darby further believed that the third temple would be rebuilt during this period and Old Testament sacrificial practices reinstated, but only as symbols of Christ's great sacrifice, which was to be the actual, but unrecognised means of salvation for Jews post-rapture. If this was Darby's thinking, it could be seen as an extension of one aspect of Calvin's covenant theology. Calvin believed that prior to Christ's work on the cross the Israelites materially approached God with animal sacrifices, but ultimately they were being saved through the blood of Christ

---

[56] Wilkinson, Op. cit., pp. 114-5

where God's grace was at work before the actual event. The temple was necessary, Darby thought, because the antichrist would one day seek to take it over, thus committing the prophesised abomination that causes desolation.[57] Under this theological scheme then the Christian Church would be spared the terrors of the great tribulation, but the Jews as a nation would not be spared with only a remnant surviving until the end.

The problem as I see it for the dispensationalist theology of Darby is that it seeks to hide from Jews what has been revealed to them in Scripture openly. It seeks to deny Jews the opportunity for a heavenly blessing that Scripture clearly teaches is their inheritance through Abraham, and this for the reason of offering Jews a lesser earthly blessing and great earthly suffering. By seeking to deny the full blessing of Abraham to Jews, it teaches that Jews are to go through another great tribulation alone, and this following the terrors of the holocaust in the twentieth century and two thousand years of Jewish suffering. It also seeks to divide Jews from Gentiles, when Scripture clearly teaches that God has united them both as part of a common plan for all humanity through the Church.

Calvin's theology also involved unity for Jews and Gentiles in Christ, and God's plan is to bring blessing and unity to all people through the promise given to Abraham. It is interesting to note that Pawson also rejects the dispensationalist theology of Darby in favour of what he calls classic Zionism, which he believes is the traditional view of evangelicals pre-Darby.[58] However, while I think this is a move in the right direction, questions remain about whether Christians should be involved in supporting Zionism as a nationalistic, political movement.

There is also a question about the misappropriation of language, as those opposed to Darby's dispensationalism have

---

[57] Wilkinson, Op. cit., pp. 128-131 [It may be argued instead that this event took place between AD 67-70 just prior to the destruction of the temple.]
[58] Pawson, Op. cit.

nothing against the broad concept that God pours out various covenantal dispensations of grace at different times. That was standard Brethren teaching without association with Israel, and it is similar to covenant type theology. The same with Zionism; many Old Testament prophecies relating to Jesus ministry (*Isa. 35: 1-10*) speak of Zion as spiritual Israel, in fact one of my favourite hymns as a child was Isaac Watts' 'We are marching to Zion,' which many found uplifting in celebrating the beauty of the New Jerusalem without considering an earthly state of Israel separately from Christ.

Benjamin Wills Newton and the Open Brethren

Sadly, the dispensationalist theology of Darby was partly responsible for the split between the early Brethren movement into Open and Exclusive groupings, although questions over Brethren governance and a power struggle were also seemingly to blame. At face value though divisions caused by disagreement over the timing of the rapture, whether pre or post, seem remarkably trivial and quite perverse, but it really involved a fundamental question relating to the extent of Christ's sacrificial work of grace. In other words, it seemed to involve a different gospel for Israel than the gospel for Christians, and thus it downplayed the centrality of the message for Jews. The gospel was then increasingly seen as being necessary for Gentiles only.

Oxford graduate and influential Brethren preacher Benjamin Wills Newton openly questioned Darby's eschatology and did not attend the 1834 Powerscourt meeting as a result, apparently disagreeing with Darby over the timing and purpose of the rapture. As noted, Darby believed the Christian Church could be raptured at any moment with the unconverted Jews then left to fulfil God's purposes on earth by going through the great tribulation alone, together with a newly constructed temple and the reintroduction of old covenant practices. Newton though was coming to see that the return of Christ and the rapture could not happen until after the conversion of Jews and restoration of the Israelite nation as part of the Christian Church, and that both Jewish and Gentile believers would go through the tribulation together under the new covenant. As such, certain things had to happen first before Christ would return. Both men wrote an increasingly acrimonious series of pamphlets. In the early 1840s Newton considered Darby's theology of dispensationalism to be a serious departure from sound theology because it implied that Jews could be reconciled to God apart from Christ's sacrificial work on the cross, and claimed that Darby was practically giving up on Christianity. Other leading Brethren such as George Muller of the Bristol based Bethesda fellowship and Henry Craik also rejected dispensationalist theology on similar grounds, even though Muller had at one time been an enthusiastic supporter of the work of the LSPCJ, and had come to Britain to train as an evangelist to Jews with the organisation. Samuel Tregelles, a notable Brethren teacher also opposed the dispensationalism of Darby, commenting in *The Christian Annotator* in 1855 that Christians should be looking for the final advent, not a secret rapture accusing those who proposed such notions of being 'Judaisers.'[59]

While in Switzerland, Darby was concerned about the growing influence that Newton had within the Brethren movement and accused him of clericalism, a charge that was heard by a council of thirteen in April 1845. Newton was acquitted of this charge, but the actual cause of the split between Darby's exclusive Plymouth grouping and the more open Bethesda assembly was to do with an erroneous pamphlet that Newton had written concerning the humanity of Christ in 1847. Although Newton quickly admitted and repented of his error, Darby rejected Newton's apology and used it to destroy Newton's reputation and also attempted to isolate Bethesda by putting the whole Church out of fellowship with his own

---

[59] Tregelles, S.P., '*Premillennial Advent*' The Christian Annotator, June 16, 1855, p. 190.

grouping for allegedly accepting Newton's heresy and refusing to deal with Newton's errors. The fact that Muller and Bethesda had rejected Newton's theological musing from the beginning and accepted Newton's quick repentant apology meant that Darby's continued attack was a cause of further division. Thus, while the repentant Newton was ostracised, and Bethesda considered heretical by Darby's group, Darby continued to promote widely his own theology that Newton had considered to be a partial denial of Christ's work on the cross.[60] It does not take too much imagination to wonder whether these side issues that were raised against Newton by Darby and friends were because of Newton's disagreement with Darby's theology and because his growing influence was seen as a threat. Incidentally, it may be noted that the Open Brethren prospered more than the Exclusive group because of their greater openness with a devolved authority amongst the assemblies providing local autonomy.

Scofield

This new theological framework of dispensationalism was later popularised through Cyrus Scofield's with his well-known Scofield Reference Bible in the early twentieth century. This biblical commentary had up to seven dispensations of grace noted. The Anglican adopted LSPCJ was also developing more as a vehicle for promoting Christian Zionism and dispensationalist theology than seeking to provide a platform for converting Jews to Christ. In fact it is noteworthy that the development of Christian Zionism has been closely associated with this organisation from the beginning of the nineteenth century, even though at first it did not take an official line. The difficulty for those who have been taught the dispensationalist theology comes in trying to marry up this particular view of

---

[60] This account comes from; Steer, R. *George Muller*, Christian Focus Publications, 1997, pp. 104-111

eschatology with the teaching of the New Testament, especially Pauline doctrine in the letters to the Romans, Galatians, Ephesians and also in the letter to the Hebrews; although it must be said in response to this that not all supporters of Christian Zionism hold to the more extreme views. Many Christian Zionists believe that God has restored a Jewish state so that, in time, there will be a mass revival for Jews with conversion to Christ under the new covenant before he returns.[61]

Development of Political Zionism

The first Zionist Congress was held in 1897 in Basel in Switzerland where the leader of the Zionist movement, Theodor Herzl, commented in his diary of the 29th August that at this meeting he was able to establish the Jewish State, and that within fifty years everyone will see it. Exactly fifty years later in 1947 on the same date of 29th August, the United Nations General Assembly passed a resolution by 33 votes to 13 in favour of the partition of Palestine and within a year the State of Israel was born in May 1948.[62] The Balfour Declaration of the 2nd November 1917 had also promised that 'His Majesty's Government views with favour the establishment in Palestine of a national home for Jewish people...'

It is further believed by proponents of Zionism that God is re-establishing Israel in fulfilment of Old Testament prophecies, with supportive evidence from passages such as *Ezekiel 36 to 38*, where the dry bones are said to come back to life as pre-signifying Israel's re-settlement in the land of Canaan. Another favourite passage is *Isaiah 49:22* where even the Gentiles are said to carry the scattered Israelites back to the land.

---

[61] See for instance Pawson, Op. cit.
[62] See: Pearce, T., *The Omega Files*, New Wine Press, 2002, pp. 80-81

This is what the Sovereign LORD says: "See, I will beckon to the Gentiles, I will lift up my banner to the peoples; they will bring your sons in their arms and carry your daughters on their shoulders. (*Isaiah 49:22*).

In later chapters I will argue that these passages from Ezekiel and Isaiah should be interpreted in terms of their fulfilment in Christ and applicable to the northern exile of Israel, not to present dispersion of Jews.

Hal Lindsey

Hal Lindsey in *The Late Great Planet Earth*, argued that Israel was being re-established by God, but that it would then be attacked by communist Russia as representatives of Gog and Magog (from *Ezekiel 38 & 39*).[63] Wolvoord and Wolvoord develop a similar eschatology in their book *Armageddon*.[64] But the end of the Cold War led many to belief that Hal Lindsey was probably wrong and others have looked elsewhere for the antichrist; contenders included various rulers of Islamic countries with Islam considered the main threat to Israel in the present day. Further interest has come through Tim La Haye's *Left Behind* series of books. As noted previously, what is often overlooked is that some forms of Christian Zionism require the State of Israel to be re-established because it is believed that Israel is a central player in the end time battle of Armageddon. In this interpretation only 144,000 Jews will survive the battle, with the Israelis experiencing another holocaust. Of course most Christians are powerless to stop the unfolding of history in human terms with little political influence, but it is highly questionable whether Christians with greater political influence should engage in activity to bring about a series of events that

---

[63] Lindsey, H. *The Late Great Planet Earth*, Zondervan, 1974, p.152
[64] Wolvoord J.F. and Wolvoord J.E. *Armageddon: Oil and the Middle East Crisis,* Zondervan Press, 1974

are based upon an incomplete understanding of eschatology, especially when so many Jews are then placed in great danger. Instead, Christian political activity should be focused on the two great commissions; firstly to be good stewards of the earth, and secondly to spread the gospel message of God's saving love that goes out to all nations and to all mankind irrespective of their ethnic identity. To try and make prophecy happen through human endeavour outside of God's grace is really to manipulate God and is a form of unbelief. Some Jewish leaders have also expressed concern that extreme Christian Zionism is hindering the peace process with Palestinians, and further entails another holocaust for the Jewish people.

The growth in Zionism is also causing concern amongst Palestinian Christians. In recent times, the leading clergy in Jerusalem released the Jerusalem Declaration on Christian Zionism on the 22nd August 2006 in order to counter Christian Zionism. In this statement the Patriarch and local heads of the churches in Jerusalem called for an end to militarism and for Christians to work towards peace and for the healing of the nations. They further asserted that God has reconciled himself to the world through Christ (*2 Cor. 5: 19*) and observed that Christian Zionism is a 'modern theological and political movement' that is really an ideology containing false teaching. This new doctrine they claim corrupts the gospel of God's 'love, justice and reconciliation' and replaces it with a worldview based on 'empire, colonialism and militarism.' (The full text is given in Appendix 1).

It would seem as well that the appeal of Zionism and the attraction of the restoration of a state called Israel amongst Christians, has much to do with it being an extension of the apologetic value of the continuation of the Jews as noted by Augustine. Some Christians are excited by Israel because they see it as a fulfilment of prophecy and a confirmation of their own faith, where history is seen to be playing out according to a divine plan. The existence of Israel then fills a confirmatory need in some Christians. However, the Bible teaches that faith comes as a gift of the Holy Spirit who provides revelation of the person of Jesus Christ to the believer. The problem is though that in a Christian's excitement it is easy to fall into error if the evidence is not properly evaluated against Scripture. The New Testament writers noted on a number of occasions not to get carried away with whims of doctrine and warned against false teachers who were trying to get into the flock. The two main concerns were from those who wanted to take the Christian community back to legalistic Judaism, and the other threat came from pagan sources such as neo-Platonism and Gnosticism.

But what does modern-day Christian Zionism actually teach? While the more extreme views are often not stated, and clearly not held by all, it is worth noting and reviewing the most basic beliefs of Christian Zionism. In February 1996 the Third International Christian Zionist Congress in Jerusalem issued a declaration with five main points that may be seen as representative of the bulk of views in this area; as follows:

1. God the Father, Almighty, chose the ancient nation and people of Israel, the descendants of Abraham, Isaac and Jacob, to reveal His plan of redemption for the world. They remain elect of God, and without the Jewish nation His redemptive purposes for the world will not be completed.
2. Jesus of Nazareth is the Messiah and has promised to return to Jerusalem, to Israel and to the world.
3. It is reprehensible that generations of Jewish peoples have been killed and persecuted in the name of our Lord, and we challenge the Church to repent of any sins of commission or omission against them.
4. The modern ingathering of the Jewish People to Eretz Israel and the rebirth of the nation of Israel are in fulfillment of biblical prophecies, as written in both Old and New Testaments.
5. Christian believers are instructed by Scripture to acknowledge the Hebraic roots of their faith and to actively assist and participate in the plan of God for the ingathering

of the Jewish People and the Restoration of the nation of Israel in our day.

These claims will be reviewed and discussed in detail as we go through subsequent chapters. Another main protagonist at the present time for Christian Zionism is John Hagee, who was written many books on the subject. We will look in detail at some of the statements of Hagee as well later, but first it is worth looking at what the Bible (especially the Old Testament prophets and New Testament writers) has to say about these issues. There is in fact a great deal of teaching in the Old and New Testament that is generally overlooked, but it is, I believe, of utmost importance to study this subject in greater depth, but also to research it in its proper historical context taking into account the blessings of Abraham, Isaac and Jacob-Israel.

Chapter 4

Israel in the Old Testament Prophets

An important question to ask is how the Christian Church relates to Israel. Can it really be shown that the Church is the legitimate continuation of Judah and Israel, together with Gentiles, and if so in what sense? Before answering this question it needs to be acknowledged that there is confusion over use of the name Israel in the Bible. Sometimes Israel refers to the northern tribes, especially Joseph and Ephraim in exile, at other times it refers to united Judah and Israel, at other times it refers to the remnant of Jews; that is those of the tribe of Judah who lived in Palestine at the time of Christ. Today, people use the name Israel for the State of Israel, or the Jews as a people, without considering that the majority in the state today identify themselves as Jews, and not those who the Old Testament prophets generally considered to be Israelites, those of the exiled northern tribes who, at face value, did not return to the land. Pawson for instance makes this error in his recent book, commenting that the first exile experienced by the Israelites was that of the Babylonian captivity, with the second exile occurring following their rejection of Christ. Thus he completely ignores the exile of the northern ten tribes by the Assyrians around 721BC, and misses the scriptural promises of restoration to those who were truly Israelites in the Old Testament.[65]

Before we get into the chapter fully it is worth looking at the promises relating to Joseph and Ephraim, and also the prophetic blessing that Jacob–Israel spoke over them. Firstly, it is worth noting that Ephraim and Manasseh were born to an Egyptian mother Asenath, and it is of interest that Ephraim was named because God had made Joseph fruitful (*Gen. 41: 42, 52*). Jacob especially blessed both Joseph, and his sons Ephraim and

---

[65] Pawson, Op.cit., pp. 97-99

Manasseh, with the desire that they be known after Abraham, Isaac and Jacob-Israel and that their offspring would spread across the earth (*Gen. 48: 15-16*). Incidentally, Ephraim was Joseph's second born son, but his blessing would exceed that of his older brother. The longer blessing for Joseph is found in *Gen. 49: 22-26*. According to this passage, Joseph was blessed to become a fruitful vine planted by a spring (fruitfulness being an important part of God's blessing) and his branches would spread over a wall, i.e. extend into other nations. His arm will be steady in the face of battle, and Jacob-Israel said that all of his blessings would rest upon Joseph who would become a 'prince among his brothers.' Reuben would then no longer be the first because of his sin. In other words, Joseph and his sons were to possess the birthright of Israel (*1 Chron. 5: 1-2*). However, the sceptre, the promised ruler, was to come through Judah (*Gen. 49: 10*).

When reading the prophets care needs to be given to understand which Israelite group the prophets were referring to, and therefore avoid false interpretations by applying prophecies relating to the northern tribes of Israel to Judah. I would urge the reader then to consider the following discussion about the Old Testament prophets carefully in what I believe to be the correct context; that is by considering which Israel the prophets were referring to. Although occasionally Judah is considered a remnant of Israel, the prophets are clear that God had not forgotten the northern tribes, and therefore they had a continued divine calling even in exile, often being identified after Ephraim and Joseph. This northern Israel was promised reunification with Judah, under a new covenant, and under 'David' the coming Judaic Messiah.

What I believe Scripture clearly teaches is that the Church should be considered a legitimate continuation, or extension of a united Israel and Judah, in a spiritual, ethnic and legal sense. This comes out of the Old Testament prophets as will be shown in this chapter. There is a danger in over emphasising the spiritual dimension at the expense of the literal, and some of those who teach against Christian Zionism fail to fully appreciate an interpretive framework where significant theology is interwoven with real physical people and events. If we fail to recognise this we are in danger of creating a false dualism where everything is spiritualised until it has no meaning in the physical world. There is a need therefore to address the Scriptures that speak of a return of Israel to the land of Palestine both in a literal as well as a spiritual sense. However, on the other side of the fence there is the danger of applying a false literalism to Scripture where the words of the text are fitted into an interpretative framework that doesn't respect the historical and cultural context. I believe that Christian Zionists are right to argue that the Old Testament Scriptures, which speak of a return of Israel to the land, need a literal interpretation, but they are wrong in their interpretation because of a failure to understand the historical and theological context correctly. What I think is evident, and I hope to show it in subsequent chapters, is that the Old Testament prophets were speaking of a return of the ten northern tribes of Israel to the land in both a literal and a spiritual sense, united together with Judah's tribe (and the Gentiles), but under the promised Messiah, Jesus Christ.

Furthermore, most of the disciples were Jews and formed a legitimate, lawfully established Jewish community. However, what will be shown is that these Jewish disciples took the message of the kingdom to the Israelites, both during, and after Christ's ministry on earth, thus reuniting Judah and Israel according to God's promises in the Old Testament. Therefore Gentile converts were assimilated into an essentially Jewish and Israelite ethnic mix and identity through conversion (and later intermarriage), and gradually that Jewish culture became more and more foreign in outward appearance, although it remained Jewish and Israelite in terms of its heritage and root.

The early Church was also related to Abraham's children through the spiritual aspect of faith. An important point to remember is that the true children of Abraham are those who have faith in Christ. Therefore true Israelites will be identified by their faith because of the promise of God and it is not simply a matter of birth. Paul noted in *Romans*, quoting the Old Testament prophets, that 'not all who are descended from Israel are Israel,' but only those born according to God's promise, which comes by faith (*Rom. 9: 6-9*). It is necessary therefore to look at a number of the Old Testament prophets to see what their preaching entailed. A clear consistent message emerges that is in harmony with the later teachings of the New Testament writers; that the northern exiled Israelites too would be restored and reunited with the tribes of Judah and Benjamin under the authority of the coming Messiah (The southern tribes also contained those of the priestly tribe Levi, and some from the tribe of Simeon who were assimilated into Judah and Benjamin). But also this promise of God would extend to the Gentiles as the small land of Palestine would be too small to hold them all.

Amos

Amos was one of the earlier prophets, writing during the early and mid part of the eighth century BC, around 760 to 750 BC, more specifically to the northern kingdom of Israel. Through a series of visions, God promised, through Amos, to rebuild Israel after a period of judgment and exile. The house of Israel is promised that it will not be totally destroyed, but shaken by God amongst the nation (*Amos 9: 8-9*). 'David's fallen tent' will be rebuilt and repaired 'as it used to be' and Israel will possess the remnant of Edom, and the 'nations that bear my name' (*Amos 9: 11-12*). This is the passage that James appeals to (*Acts 15: 16-17*) when the apostles bring news to Jerusalem that Gentiles are converting to Christ. Amos further asserts that the 'reaper will be overtaken by the ploughman,' and new wine will drip from the mountains, as God says that he will bring back the exiled people of Israel who will be planted in their own land, never again to be uprooted at the same time as the Gentiles are being brought in (*Amos 9: 13-15*).

Hosea

Hosea was from the northern part of Israel, and prophesied in the latter part of the eighth century BC identifying Assyria as God's instrument to judge Israel. The exile of the northern tribes took place in 721 BC and is recorded in *2 Kings 17: 6*; 'The King of Assyria captured Samaria, and deported the Israelites to Assyria. He settled them in Halah, in Gozan on the Habor River, and in the towns of the Medes.'

Paul quotes from Hosea in Romans (*Rom. 9: 25-27*), and notes that God said that he would save a remnant of Jews, and then call a people who were not his natural people, sons of the living God (*Hos. 1: 10; Hos. 2: 23*). From the Old Testament prophets it can be seen that it was God's plan to graft Gentile believers into the Jewish root, but also to re-graft the nations of exiled Israel into the olive rootstock as well. According to Hosea, God's plan was to make the Israelites as numerous as the sand on the seashore and therefore beyond measure (*Hos 1: 10*). The land of Palestine could never hold such a number of people, and it was always God's plan for the seed of Abraham to be sown, or scattered, into the world and thus be a blessing to all nations.

Hosea, writing during the time just prior to the northern exile, is commanded by God to take an adulterous woman called Gomer to be his wife as symbolic of the adultery of Israel (*Hos. 1: 2-3*). Hosea then names his children according to the prophetic plan of God. The first son was called Jezreel, meaning God scatters, because God planned to break the kingdom of Israel and bring it to an end scattering (sowing) the Israelites amongst the nations. The second daughter was named Lo-Ruhamah because God would no longer show love to Israel, although Judah would find love and be saved as a nation for the purpose of bringing forth the promised leader, this according to God's sovereignty and power. The third son was named Lo-Ammi, and while God had rejected the Israelites, they are told they would become very numerous indeed (*Hos. 1: 4-9*).

Reunion is then promised between Judah and Israel under one ruler, but the Israelites will have become as numerous as the sand on the seashore (*Hos. 1: 10-11*). In the next chapter, we see Hosea elaborate further on how God would deal with the people of Israel. First of all God says that he would divorce Israel and then send her away because of her sin (*Hos. 2: 2-7*). However, in Israel's wanderings she would fail to find satisfaction with foreign lovers (foreign deities) and thus desire to be reunited with God. God then promised to 'allure' Israel again and show love to her bringing her through the desert and removing the worship and invocation of Baal from her lips, and Israel was promised that she would again call upon God as 'my husband' and not 'my master' (*Hos. 2: 14-17*). God further promises to remarry Israel through a new covenant that will last forever based on righteousness and justice, love and compassion (*Hos. 2: 14-20*). In Isaiah a young wife who had been divorced was also to be brought back with deep compassion (*Isa. 54: 5-10*). Fruitfulness and prosperity are then promised, as is the promise of restoration where the Israelites who were rejected and unloved by God would again be called 'my people' and they would identify themselves as God's people (*Hos. 2: 21-23*). There is then reunification between Judah and Israel within the new covenant, and thus remarriage to God is promised on a new basis. Although the Israelites will live without a king or prince for many days, in the last days they will return and seek God and 'David' (Jesus) their king (*Hos. 3: 4-5*).

Isaiah

Isaiah's ministry began in 740 BC, before the northern Israelite exile and also therefore before the Judean exile, but he continued to minister through the period of the northern exile until around 681 BC. He was therefore a contemporary of Micah, Amos and Hosea and prophesied to, and often against Israel, although with the hope that Israel would again be reconciled and restored in the future. Isaiah was shown that a fruitful branch, or a root, will come from Jesse and rule with wisdom and understanding as given by God's Spirit (*Isa. 11: 1-2*). The root of Jesse will become a banner for the nations and he will bring a remnant of the exiles of Israel and Judah into his rest from the four corners of the earth (*Isa. 11: 10-12*). These people will be gathered out of the nations, including those who are in Assyria, and there will then be unity between the remnant of Judah and Ephraim.[66] God then promised to make a highway for the remnant of his people who were in Assyria, but under the leadership of the root of Jesse (the Messiah) as a banner to the nations (*Isa. 11: 12-16*).

The promise of God had always been to bless the nations of the earth through the offspring of Abraham, and Isaiah commented that God would 'enlarge' the nation of Israel and 'increase' the government of the Messiah who would sit on David's throne forever (*Isa. 9: 3, 7*). Jacob is further promised compassion and resettlement in the land according to God's word, but also aliens, as the Gentile nations, would join with the Israelites in unity and together they would possess the nations (*Isa. 14: 1-2*) bringing their former captor, the king of Babylon under their feet; even the morning star, often considered to be Lucifer, would be brought down because of his pride (*Isa. 14: 3-16*). With the sins of God's people atoned for, they would then fill the world with fruit (spiritual fruit) and the pagan stones would be smashed and the Asherite poles removed from their place (*Isa. 27: 6-9*).

Isaiah *49* is often used in support of Christian Zionism, but it is addressed to the 'islands' and 'distant nations' (*Isa. 49: 1*). The first section of this chapter considers the coming Messiah, the servant of the Lord who is described as a polished arrow concealed in God's quiver, called from before his birth (*Isa. 49: 1-2*). His mouth is said to be like a sharpened sword and he is hidden in the palm of God's hand. Although God says,

---

[66] Ephraim was Joseph's son by an Egyptian mother Asenath. Ephraim though represented the northern tribes of Israel.

through Isaiah, that; 'You are my servant, Israel, in whom I will display my splendour' (*Isa. 49: 3*) this passage is not referring to Israel as being God's servant at this point because it is also stated that he (the Messiah) was born for the purpose of bringing 'Jacob back to him and [to] gather Israel to himself' (*Isa. 49: 5*). The passage is then asserting that God will display the servant's splendour through Israel and through reconciliation between Judah and Israel. However, according to the passage the gathering of Jacob and Israel on its own is considered too small a thing for the servant because he is also to be a 'light for the Gentiles' so that he 'may bring [God's] salvation to the ends of the earth' (*Isa. 49: 6*).

"This is what the LORD says - the Redeemer and Holy One of Israel - to him who was despised and abhorred by the nation, to the servant of rulers: "Kings will see you and rise up, princes will see and bow down, because of the LORD, who is faithful, the Holy One of Israel, who has chosen you." (*Isa. 49: 7*).

The Lord further promises to make the servant to be a 'covenant for the people' to 'restore the land' to bring the captives out and set them free.

"In the time of my favour I will answer you, and in the day of salvation I will help you; I will keep you and will make you to be a covenant for the people, to restore the land and to reassign its desolate inheritances, to say to the captives, 'Come out,' and to those in darkness, 'Be free!' "They will feed beside the roads and find pasture on every barren hill. They will neither hunger nor thirst, nor will the desert heat or the sun beat upon them. He who has compassion on them will guide them and lead them beside springs of water (*Isa. 49: 8-10*).

Zion's New Name

God further says that he will turn the 'mountains into roads,' and the 'highways will be raised up' (*Isa. 49: 11*). This levelling of the ground will allow the exiles to return, coming 'from afar - some from the north, some from the west, some from the region of Aswan' (*Isa. 49: 12*).

> Shout for joy, O heavens; rejoice, O earth; burst into song, O mountains! For the LORD comforts his people and will have compassion on his afflicted ones (*Isa. 49: 13*).

God promises to remember Zion as a mother remembers her baby, and claims that he has engraved Israel in the palms of his hands and will therefore bring the sons of Israel back to the land (*Isa. 49: 14-18*). But the land will be too small for the people and they will ask God for more land (*Isa. 49: 19-20*). In other words under the new covenant the Israelites would be brought back into the land, but the land will be extended beyond the borders often considered the possession of Abraham's offspring. The Lord further promises to '...beckon to the Gentiles, I will lift up my banner to the peoples; they will bring your sons in their arms and carry your daughters on their shoulders. Kings will be your foster fathers, and their queens your nursing mothers...' (*Isa. 49: 22-23*). The captives will even be rescued as plunder from fierce warriors and the children brought to safety (*Isa. 49: 24-25*).

> Then all mankind will know that I, the LORD, am your Saviour, your Redeemer, the Mighty One of Jacob." (*Isa. 49: 26*).

The passage is really talking about the ingathering of the sons of Israel back into the land as a result of the work of Christ in the first century, but like other Old Testament prophecies, the land is stated as being too small for them. Gentiles will help in that ingathering, but the blessing that Israel receives will extend to the Gentiles and to the ends of the earth for the glory and splendour of the servant; that is Christ. Although this promise included the land of Palestine, Palestine or the 'Holy Land,' had become too small to contain the full blessings of God, and even Gentiles will take the gospel to the scattered Israelites.

God further promises that foreigners who bind themselves to the Lord will not be excluded from his people. (*Isa. 56: 3, 6*) God declares that as he gathers the exiles of Israel, so others will be gathered as well (*Isa. 56: 8*), but the blind watchmen of Israel saddened God for their lack of faithfulness, the careless shepherds who lacked knowledge and understanding. (*Isa. 56: 9-12*). However, God said that he was going to give Zion a new name, and the nations of the earth will see the glory that is given, where Zion's righteousness will 'shine like the dawn', and her salvation 'like a brazing torch' (*Isa. 62: 1-2*). No longer will Israel be deserted, but God's delight will cause him to remarry Israel, and she will become a banner to the nations (*Isa. 62: 3-11*). In Isaiah 65 a people that had not sought God will be called and found by him, but the obstinate people of God will be rejected (*Isa. 65: 1-2*). However not all the people of Jacob and Judah would be rejected, as some good fruit would be found amongst the grapes of God's people, and he will allow them to inherit the mountains of Israel in God's land. But those who have forsaken God will be rejected.

Isaiah then is consistent with other passages such as *Jeremiah 31* and *Hosea 1* (particularly Hosea) where God says that he will restore Israel, but the land will be too small to hold them all. The blessing will also extend to the Gentiles according to Hosea (and as interpreted by Paul in *Romans* (*Rom. 9-11*)). The land in these passages should be seen in light of Jesus' teaching about the kingdom of heaven spreading across the whole earth and not simply be seen as a narrow strip of land in the Middle East. No longer is God restricting his work to a single nation and small piece of land, as he did in the time of the judges and kings, but he is now fulfilling his plan to bring salvation to the ends of the earth, which was always part of God's promise given to Abraham.

It may be seen then that the global Church within the new covenant is a union between the Gentile believers and a reunion and continuation of Judah and Israel, and this is in fulfilment of the prophecies of Hosea, and Isaiah, together, as will be shown, with passages in Ezekiel, Zechariah, Jeremiah and Amos, although this study of the prophets is not exhaustive. Unlike Judah, the northern tribes of Israel did not appear to return to the land after their period of exile in any real sense, but settled in the surrounding nations where they received the gospel and entered the kingdom of heaven, which was legitimately Israel in a spiritual and legal sense (because of Joseph's birthright, and God's calling upon a remnant of Judah with Christ as King). Although that is not yet the full story as will be discussed further.

Micah

Micah too was prophesying during the second half of the eight century BC as a contemporary of Isaiah and Hosea. He predicted the fall of Israel to the Assyrians, and condemned the leaders of Judah and Israel 'who build Zion with bloodshed, and Jerusalem with wickedness' (*Mic. 3: 10*), but after a period of judgement, deliverance and restoration to the land is promised. God promised to gather the remnant of Israel and bring them together as a flock of sheep where 'their king will pass through before them, the Lord at their head' (*Mic. 2: 12-13*). In the last days, God says through Micah, the mountain of God's temple will be established and become a place of hope and teaching for the nations, where the 'law will go out from Zion' (*Mic. 4: 1-2*). As a result of this there will be peace amongst the nations where swords will be beaten into ploughshares, and 'nation will not take up sword against nation' neither will they 'train for war any more' (*Mic. 4: 3*).

Despite a temporary judgement against Israel, God promises to gather the exiles, and the lame will be turned into a strong nation and the Lord will rule over them in Mount Zion (*Mic. 4: 6-7*). Israel will be ruled over by a king who will come out of Bethlehem 'whose origins are from of old, from ancient times' *Mic. 5: 2*). Although Micah asserts that Israel will be temporarily abandoned, a time will come when Israel will return and be restored, and the ruler will 'shepherd the flock in the strength of the Lord' (*Mic. 5: 3-4*). Israel will then live in security and the greatness of the shepherd 'will reach to the ends of the earth, and he will be their peace' (*Mic. 5: 4-5*). It is noteworthy then that the new nation of Israel under the shepherd Jesus Christ will be concerned with establishing peace across the whole world and not seeking to expand through war in a small part of the Middle East.

Jeremiah

Jeremiah was from a priestly line and his ministry covered a period from 626 BC to around 586 BC. This was after the northern tribes had been taken into captivity by the Assyrians, but prior to and during the southern exile of Judah in Babylon. Jeremiah was then primarily writing against the sins of Judah and warning of God's judgment. However, Jeremiah also speaks of future restoration for both Judah and Israel under the righteous messianic shepherd.

'The days are coming declares the Lord, when I will raise up to David a righteous branch, a King who will reign wisely and do what is just and right in the land.

In his day Judah will be saved and Israel will live in safety.

This is the name by which he will be called: The Lord Our Righteousness' (*Jer. 23: 5-6*).

Jeremiah then notes that in a future time people will no longer say 'As surely as the Lord lives who brought the descendents up out of Egypt,' but they will say, 'As surely as the Lord lives who brought the descendents up out of the land of the north, and out of all the countries where he had banished them.' The people will then live in their own land (*Jer. 23: 7-8*). In other words the promised shepherd king of David's line will gather both Judah and Israel, with Israel gathered out of the north from the places where the Israelites had been exiled and scattered by the Assyrians.

Jeremiah further expands on the restoration of Israel and Judah in a lengthy discourse (*Jer. 30-33*). Both Judah and Israel are promised restoration to the land of their forefathers (*Jer. 30: 1-4*). No longer will Jacob or Israel be enslaved, but they will be brought out of a distance land and be given peace and security where they will serve the 'Lord their God and David their king' (*Jer. 30: 8-10*). God will 'restore the fortunes of Jacob's tents' and have compassion on them; the city will be rebuilt with songs of rejoicing and thanksgiving heard as God 'adds to their numbers' (*Jer. 30: 17-19*)

Jeremiah further notes that God loves the clans of Israel with an everlasting love and that they will be built up again and therefore he will allow the people to rejoice and plant vineyards on the hills of Samaria (*Jer. 31: 1-6*). Samaria was, incidentally, the area where the northern tribes (not Judah) had lived prior to their exile; the capital city also had the same name. Jeremiah says further that the people of Israel will be brought out of the land of the north and from the ends of the earth to settle in their own land (*Jer. 31: 8*), God will make the paths level alongside streams of water for 'Ephraim…my first born son,' and they will come with weeping and prayer as they return, and God promises he will be like a shepherd to the scattered flock of Israel (*Jer. 31: 9-10*). They will then rejoice in the bounty of Zion as they settle in the land (*Jer. 31: 12*). God says that he will hear the cries of distress from Ephraim, and acknowledged their repentance, and Jeremiah, in a dream, hears God call for roads signs to be set up for Israel's return (*Jer. 31: 18-21*). Both the house of Judah and the house of Israel will be planted in the land (*Jer. 31: 27*). God then promises to make a new covenant with the house of Israel and Judah, a prophecy that is quoted by the writer to the Hebrews (*Heb. 8: 8-12; Jer. 31: 31-34*).

"The time is coming," declares the LORD, "when I will make a new covenant with the house of Israel and with the house of Judah.

It will not be like the covenant I made with their forefathers when I took them by the hand to lead them out of Egypt, because they broke my covenant, though I was a husband to them," declares the LORD.

"This is the covenant I will make with the house of Israel after that time," declares the LORD. "I will put my law in their minds and write it on their hearts. I will be their God, and they will be my people.

No longer will a man teach his neighbour, or a man his brother, saying, 'Know the LORD,' because they will all know me, from the least of them to the greatest," declares the LORD. "For I will forgive their wickedness and will remember their sins no more."

God further says that the descendents of Israel will never cease to be a nation before him, as long as the sun, moon and stars endure (*Jer. 31: 35-37*). Jeremiah further prophesies that Israel will be re-gathered to a place where they can live in safety. God will give them a heart to fear and serve him faithfully, this through an everlasting covenant that God will put in place (*Jer. 32: 37-41*). The promise given in chapter 23 (*Jer. 23: 5-6*) is repeated in chapter 33 (*Jer. 33: 15-16*) with the addition that David will never cease to have a man sit on the throne of Israel (*Jer. 33: 17*), and that God's covenant with him (Jesus) can never be broken, and that priests will minister continually before God.

Zion's New Name

Ezekiel

According to Ezekiel God had not forgotten the exiled Israelites in the subsequent centuries of the Old Testament period and there are a number of prophecies relating specifically to the northern tribes of Israel, and not to Judah, although these prophecies are found in some of the less colourful parts of the Old Testament and therefore often overlooked. Ezekiel though has much to say about these northern tribes of Israel and was writing more than one hundred and twenty years after their exile. Ezekiel's prophetic ministry was carried out under the exile of the southern tribes of Judah in Babylon and he began his ministry after 597 BC, lasting some twenty years.

According to Ezekiel, Israel as a nation was to remain subject to the Assyrian authorities for several hundred years. During his ministry, Ezekiel is told by God to perform a rather odd symbolic act whereby he is commanded to lie on his left side for 390 days in order to bear the sin of the house of Israel (*Ezek. 4: 1-5*). Under this act the days were symbolic of years (*Eze. 4: 5*). The reason this is specifically a sign for Israel is because Ezekiel is next told to lie on his right side for 40 days to bear the sins of the house of Judah (*Ezek. 1: 4- 6*). What is of further interest is that the house of Israel went into exile under the Assyrians in 721 BC, and they were slaves in Assyria for 390 years until the forces of Alexander the Great finally destroyed the power of their captors in 331 BC. Assyria generally lay to the north and northeast of Israel in what is today Lebanon and Syria. The Babylonians later conqueror Assyria in 609 BC, driving the Assyrians and their captives further north and east, and 70 years later the Persians took over in 539 BC, but the northern tribes were not released at that time from their captivity. Following their final release in 331 BC, the Assyrian Israelite captives scattered to the northwest to Asia Minor and to the east. What is clear though is that God had not forgotten the northern tribes of Israel that were in exile.

Ezekiel had further prophecies regarding the house of Israel, where for instance the lost tribes were considered as a flock of neglected sheep without a shepherd (*Ezek. 34: 1-31*). In this prophecy, God lamented the lack of faithful shepherds over the flock of Israel and noted that as a result they had been scattered over the hills and mountains of the whole earth with no one to search for them (*Ezek. 34: 1-6*). As a result God himself promised to search for the lost sheep that had been scattered (*Ezek. 34: 11-12*) and bring them back into the land, pasturing them on the mountains of Israel (*Ezek. 34: 13-16*). God also promised to protect them from plunder and judge fairly between the sheep, placing over them the faithful shepherd 'David' (*Ezek. 34: 17-24*). The prophecy goes on to assert that God would make a covenant of peace with the house of Israel and bless their land with fruitful abundance (*Ezek. 34: 25-31*).

Prophecies concerning the house of Israel, and the promise of the reunion of Judah and Israel continue through *Ezekiel 36* and *37*. God promised to bless Israel by removing them from the surrounding nations and therefore to bring them back into their own land, this for the sake of his own holy name in spite of their unfaithfulness (*Ezek. 36: 23-24*). God then promised to cleanse the people from their impurities with the sprinkling of clean water and by giving them a 'new heart' and a 'new spirit' (*Ezek. 36: 25-26*). In this regard God promised that his Spirit would be in them and they would then be moved to obedience, (*Ezek. 36: 27*) with the further promise of fruitfulness and great increase in number. In *Ezekiel 37: 1-10* the dry bones are seen to come back to life where tendons, skin and muscles are added, then God breathes life into the body. These bones are representative of the 'whole house of Israel' where God promises to place his Spirit within them as they are settled in their own land; that is in Christ (*Ezek. 37: 11-14*).

In the second part of *Ezekiel 37 (Ezek. 37: 15-28)* both Israel and Judah are promised reunification under one king. Ezekiel is told to take a stick and write on it 'Belonging to Judah and the Israelites associated with him' and then to take another stick and write 'Ephraim's stick, belonging to Joseph and all the house of Israel associated with him.' Then Ezekiel is told to join the two together in his hand (*Ezek. 37: 15-17*). The promise here is that God is going to bring back into the land of Israel all his people, both the people of Judah and the northern tribes of Israel, and join them together so that they will never be divided again, and also to save them from their sin (*Ezek. 37: 18-23*). The promise is further given that they will then dwell in the land of Jacob under the great shepherd-king David, forever with a great increase in number, and God further promised to make a covenant of peace with them that will be an everlasting covenant and the nations will see that it is the Lord who makes Israel holy (*Ezek. 37: 24-28*). This was fulfilled in the time of Christ and the apostles. As noted, there are other prophecies in the Old Testament that speak of God making a covenant under one ruler with a reunited Israel and Judah (*Hos. 1: 11*; *Jer. 31: 31; Jer. 50: 4-6*).

God further promises to have compassion on all the people of Israel bringing Jacob back from captivity, where God will pour out his Spirit upon the house of Israel (*Ezek. 39: 23-29*).[67] In the following chapters (*Ezek. 40-46*), Ezekiel sees a new temple being built where God will live amongst the Israelites forever (*Ezek. 43: 7*) (The writer to the Hebrews later identifies the body of Christ as the temple). Ezekiel (*Ezek. 47*) then sees a river flowing out of the east gate of the temple towards the Dead Sea, that will be a life giving blessing to all it touches, and it was too deep to cross. Trees will grow along the banks of the river, and fish will live in the Dead Sea.[68]

---

[67] In Ezekiel chapters 38 and the first part of 39, after a period of 'many days' and in 'future years' Gog and Magog will be summoned against a people who live in safety on the mountains of Israel, a people gathered out of the nations, but God will bring judgement against Gog.

[68] The apostle John also saw a vision of the New Jerusalem coming down from heaven where the Lord Almighty and the Lamb are the temple together with a river flowing out from the throne of the lamb to be a blessing to all nations (*Rev. 21-22*).

Zion's New Name

Zechariah

Zechariah was a contemporary of Haggai and his ministry continued from around 520 BC to around 480 BC. From a priestly line, he had returned with the exiles from Babylon in 538 BC, and thus his ministry covered a period just before, and immediately after the restoration of Judah, but prior to the foreseen restoration of Israel. Zechariah begins by speaking about the return of Judah to the land, but also mentions that those scattered in the north will be brought back, that is the exiles forced out by the Assyrians (*Zech. 2: 6*), together with many nations joining with the Lord to become God's people (*Zech. 2: 11*). This Zion is also described as the apple of God's eye (*Zech. 2: 8*).

With Judah restored Zechariah also sees God 'saving the house of Joseph' and restoring them in his compassion (*Zech. 10: 6*). The Ephraimites too will be gathered back to the land, and become as numerous as before, being brought out of Egypt and Assyria (*Zech. 10: 6-12*). God promised to save Judah and Israel and make them a blessing (*Zech. 8: 13*) then Zechariah sees the coming king bringing righteousness and salvation in gentleness and humility even riding on 'the foal of a donkey' (*Zech. 9: 9*), but in his grace and might taking away the 'chariots from Ephraim' and the 'war horses from Jerusalem' (*Zech. 9: 10*). He will further proclaim peace to the nations, extending his rule to the ends of the earth where by his covenant of blood he will set the prisoners free. Judah will become as a bow with Ephraim the arrows in God's quiver (*Zech. 9: 11-13*). God in his meekness and majesty will rule over the whole earth through a union of Judah and Israel where his arrows will flash like the lightning (*Zech. 9: 10-14*). Zechariah further hears God promising to become a shepherd to Judah where the ruler will be the cornerstone of his people and empower them to overcome their enemies (*Zech. 10: 1-5*). God further promises to strengthen and save the house of Joseph as well as the house of Judah, with the people gathered back into the land and greatly increasing in number, being brought back from Egypt and Assyria (*Zech. 10: 6-12*).

However, just as Zechariah sees reunion between Judah and Israel and resettlement under the good shepherd, he also sees further division for rebellion and observes that one flock will be marked for slaughter for unfaithfulness towards God. In their rebellion they paid the shepherd the price of thirty pieces of silver and God revoked his old covenant with them (*Zech. 11: 4-17*) breaking his two staffs marked Favour and Union. The shepherd who is close to the Lord would be struck by the sword and taken away from them because they had turned against him and as a result the sheep would be scattered with two-thirds falling into judgement (*Zech. 13: 7-8*).

However, one-third of the united Judah and Israel was promised strengthening at the hands of the shepherd where they would be refined by fire as silver and gold and as a result the people would acknowledge God, and God would hear their prayers (*Zech. 13: 8-9*). It was therefore to be through God's Spirit that he promised to pour out on the house of David a new spirit of 'grace and supplication.' This new spirit within them would then lead them to mourn for the one 'they [had] pierced' (*Zech. 12: 10-14*), and thus cleanse them from their sin (*Zech. 13: 1-2*); a prophecy fulfilled on the day of Pentecost.

Zechariah notes as well that Jerusalem is to become a cup that sends nations reeling, or a rock on which those who come against the city will be injured (*Zech. 12: 2-3*). While Christian Zionists find appeal in this passage for their particular interpretation I think instead that these verses should be interpreted in terms of the New Jerusalem; that is the Church of the first century AD, the heavenly city where the Jewish apostles should be considered the leaders of Judah. In the passage they are described as braziers in a woodpile and God says that he will save the dwellings of Judah first, with the feeblest amongst them to become like David (*Zech. 12: 6-8*). The rock is symbolic of God's kingdom smashing to pieces the idolatrous kingdoms of the world as recorded in the prophecy of Daniel (*Dan. 2: 31-35*), but as well this passage is in the context of God pouring out the Holy Spirit on the house of David with subsequent weeping for the one who was pierced. 'On that day' a fountain will be opened to cleanse the people from their sin, and the idols will be banished from the land (*Zech. 13: 1-2*).

God also says through Zechariah that he will be jealous for Zion, and return to dwell in Jerusalem, where Jerusalem will be called a 'City of Truth' and God's mountain will be considered 'Holy' (*Zech. 8: 1-3*). God will bring back a remnant of his people from the east and west (*Zech. 8: 7-8*) where both Judah and Israel will be a blessing, bearing fruit for God according to his righteous judgements (*Zech. 8: 12-14*). Powerful nations and people of different languages will seek the Lord in Jerusalem, taking hold of the righteous Jews and asking to go with them because they have heard that God is with them (*Zech. 8: 20-23*). This should be interpreted as a reference to the work of Christ in the Church, where the Jewish apostles preached first to Jews, but later Gentiles gladly joined with them, and the apostles were commanded by God not to hinder his work in saving Gentiles also.

Chapter 5

Restoring Israel to the Land

Following the northern exile of Israel, some have tried to trace the subsequent wanderings and settlements of the so-called lost tribes of Israel through Europe with a number of theories given, although much of this is speculative and only the basis for such arguments is given in Appendix 4. However, a much simpler case can be made for the unification of Judah and Israel in the early Christian period that is in accord with Old Testament prophecies. When the early Christian apostles travelled and preached many of their converts were from the northern tribes of Israel. And this work was not by accident, but instead by God's design and by deliberate action on the part of the apostles who believed they were acting under Jesus' direct commission. At the time of Christ in fact the scattered Israelites were not considered lost at all. But following conversion to Christianity their identity became linked more closely with the Christian Church that was becoming increasingly non-Jewish in outlook and culture, and therefore their separate Hebraic identity gradually disappeared. As the Christian Church re-settled Palestine in subsequent centuries, with communities and churches built, Judah and Israel re-entered and settled in the land as part of the united Christian community, but Christianity was spreading far beyond the borders of Palestine. Israel therefore did resettle the land according to God's promises in a literal sense, but not in the way Christian Zionists recognise today.

The important and interesting question here then concerns the place of settlement of the northern tribes of Israel following their exile. What happened to them and where did they go? Although it is widely assumed today that once the Israelites had gone into exile their separate identity slowly diminished to the point where they were subsumed into the surrounding cultures and effectively disappeared as a people and nation. This is certainly the view of the *Encyclopaedia Britannica*[69] and of the *Interpreter's Dictionary of the Bible.*[70] The text notes of the *New International Version Study Bible* also for instance have very little to say on this matter, and largely interpret comments relating to Israel, following the northern exile, in terms of its application to the tribe of Judah. Some Jews today recognise the problem as well believing that there are many unfulfilled promises in the Old Testament that speak of the reunion of Judah and Israel under the Messiah, but many believe the Israelite tribes have simply disappeared from history. This problem is for instance recognised in the *Jewish Encyclopaedia.*[71] But how can Scripture be fulfilled if the northern Israelite tribes have disappeared? As has been shown in the previous the prophets spoke of reunion under the Messiah.

The Old Testament prophets then are clear that the new covenant will be with both the house of Judah and the house of Israel under one shepherd who is the promised ruler of Judah; that is 'David' the Messiah, but only a part of Judah and Israel will be saved at this time. But can it be shown that this was fulfilled in the person of Jesus Christ? Did Christ come to be a shepherd to both Judah and Israel, as well as the Gentiles?

The New Testament disciples and leaders of the Church were not silent on this subject although again the text notes of the *New International Version Study Bible* overlook the significance of what was being said by Jesus and the apostles. Matthew records that Jesus sent out the twelve disciples with authority to heal the sick and drive out evil spirits (*Matt. 10: 1-5*). The disciples are commanded at this time not to go to the Samaritans or the Gentiles, but to the 'lost sheep of the house of

---

[69] Encyclopaedia .Britannica. 'Ten Lost Tribes of Israel.' Vol. 11, 1991. Some references in chapter 10 are sourced from Finch, P.R. 'Beyond Acts,' 2003.
[70] Sanders, J.A. 'Exile' in Buttrick, G.A. et al (eds.) *I.D.B.* New York: Abingdon, 1962, Vol. 2, p. 187
[71] Jacobs, J, 'Tribes, Lost Ten,' *Jewish Encyclopaedia*, ed. Singer, I., and Adler, C., New York: Funk and Wagnalls, 1925, Vol. 12: p. 249

Israel' (*Matt. 10: 6*).[72] This phrase is pointing to the fact that Jesus was acting in fulfilment of prophecy (for instance *Ezek. 34: 1-12* and *Jer. 50: 4-6*), because God had promised through these prophets to be a shepherd to the scattered sheep of the house of Israel. It also implies then that the disciples were sent out of the land of Palestine to the surrounding nations where the Israelites were then scattered by the Assyrians; that is towards the lands south of the Black Sea, the Zagros Mountain region and south of the Caspian Sea, although Jesus further commented that the disciples' ministry to the cities of Israel would not in fact be complete until he returns (*Matt. 10: 23*). It becomes clear then that the fulfilment of the Old Testament prophecies relating to Israel's restoration took place in the time of Christ and shortly afterwards, although this fulfilment would not be complete until Christ returns. While the disciples were away, Jesus taught and preached in the towns of Galilee (*Matt. 11: 1*).

Another significant passage is found in *Acts 2: 5-12*, where Luke records that there were God fearing Jews from every nation in Jerusalem for the Pentecost celebrations (*Acts 2: 5*) and they witnessed the disciples speaking in their own languages on that day, and then listened to Peter's preaching. Although Luke comments that they were Jews, the list of nations he gives is of interest because it includes the areas where the northern tribes of Israel had been scattered. Although clearly the 3000 people converted on that day did not represent all the people of Judah and Israel it was a significant first step. Firstly, there were 'Parthians and Medes' in Jerusalem (*Acts 2: 9-10*). According to the passage in *2 Kings 17: 6* the Israelites were exiled and placed in 'Halah, in Gozan on the Habor River, and in the towns of the Medes.' The later Parthian empire included areas of Media, and the Jewish historian Josephus commented in *Antiquities of the Jews* (*A.J. 11.5.2*) that the ten tribes remained beyond the Euphrates, (in the region of Media and Parthia) even

---

[72] The NIV states only 'lost sheep of Israel', but the Greek is 'lost sheep of the house [Gk oikos] of Israel' (also *Matt. 15: 24*).

until the time of Josephus, and had become an immense multitude too numerous to count.

> '...but then the entire body of the people of Israel remained in that country; wherefore there are but two tribes in Asia and Europe subject to the Romans, while the ten tribes are beyond Euphrates till now, and are an immense multitude, and not to be estimated by numbers.'[73]

Josephus in the same passage (*A.J. 11.5.2*) also comments that Esdras (Ezra) sent a copy of an epistle he had received from God to '...all those of his own nation that were in Media.' Josephus was writing for the Roman authorities and it is interesting to note that for many years the Parthian Empire was often at war with Rome. The historian George Rawlinson argued that the *Parthian* name might actually derive from a word meaning 'exile,'[74] although the root of the word is similar to the Hebrew word for 'covenant' (BRT, literally 'to fetter,' if the B is mutated into a P). The Hebrew for covenant is similar in form in the Assyrian language.[75]

Other names of places recorded in *Acts 2: 9-10* include Cappadocia, Pontus, Asia, Phyrgia and Pamphylia. The area of Pontus and Cappadocia are geographically north and west of 'Halah, Gozan and the Habor River' (from *2 Kings 17: 6*). Interestingly the Greek historian Diodorus of Sicily noted that a part of the Assyrian empire was later forced northwards settling between Pontus and Paphlagonia on the southern Black Sea

---

[73] *Antiquities of the Jews*, (11.5.2), The Works of Josephus, translated by Whiston, W., Hendrickson Publishers. 1987. 13th Printing. p. 294

[74] Rawlinson, G. *The Sixth Great Oriental Monarchy or the Geography History and Antiquities of Parthia*, New York: Dodd, Mead & Co. 1882, p.19

[75] Vine, W.E., Unger, M.F., and White W. Jr, Vine's Complete Expository Dictionary of Old and New Testament Words, Nashville: Thomas Nelson, Publ., 1985, pp. 50-51.

coast.[76] (Other parts of the Assyrian empire later extended to the northern coast of the Black Sea). It may be noted then that the people groups represented in *Acts 2: 9-10* were from areas where the Assyrians had migrated with the captive northern Israelite tribes. Having preached to these exiled believers on the day of Pentecost, Peter did not forget them, as he later wrote his first epistle to the 'chosen sojourners of the dispersion' [Gk. diasporas] of Pontus, Galatia, Cappadocia, Asia and Biythnia, chosen according to God's foreknowledge (*1 Peter 1: 1-2*). In other words, Peter was acting as God's chosen apostle to the Israelite Diaspora, which was settled in much of what is now modern Turkey. With so many converts on the day of Pentecost, the apostles would have taken records of names and addresses, and then followed up with apostolic visits. In fact they would have been negligent if they had not done so, and the fact that the book of *Acts* records the number of converts, and their places of origin, suggests they kept records.

In fact all of the disciples were chosen to be missionaries to the people of Judah and Israel first, and they preached in the lands where the 'lost' tribes dwelt. According to Acts, the disciples asked Jesus if he was going to restore the nation of Israel at that time, but Jesus' response was that they were not to know the times of such events. Instead they were to go and preach the gospel in Jerusalem, Judea and Samaria and to the ends of the earth through the power of God's Spirit (*Acts 1: 6-8*). William Cave for instance noted that Thomas took the gospel of Christ to Parthia, then to the Medes, Persians, Carmians and nations further east.[77] There is also a strong tradition that Thomas went as well to a Jewish community in Kerala, southern India. Bartholomew went to Armenia and Asia Minor, Thaddeus

---

[76] Diodorus Siculus, 'Histories,' 2:43, In *Diodorus of Sicily*, Trans. Oldfather, C.H. et al. 12 Vols. London: William Heinemann, 1933
[77] Cave, W., *A Complete History of the Lives, Acts and Martyrdom of the Holy Apostles*, Philadelphia: Solomon Wiatt, 1810, Vol. 2 p. 331

to Assyria and Mesopotamia, with Philip going to the Scythians and Upper Asia.[78]

In *Acts 2 (Acts 2: 14-39)* Peter also addressed the crowd calling them by three different titles. First of all he addresses the 'Jewish men' and the 'inhabitants of Jerusalem' and quotes from the prophet Joel (*Acts 2: 14*). Then he addresses the crowd as 'men of Israel' (*Acts 2: 22*) and quotes from David asserting that 'all the house of Israel ' should now know that Jesus is the Christ (*Acts 2: 36*). Finally Peter commented that repentance and the promise of the Holy Spirit is for 'you,' 'your children' and all those who are 'far off' (*Acts 2: 38-39*). It is noteworthy as well that the hearers of Peter's message were cut to the heart in fulfilment of Zechariah's prophecy.

James (*James 1: 1*) also mentions that he is writing as a servant in Christ to the 'twelve tribes in the dispersion' (Gk. diaspora). This is significant because of James' status as the leader of the Jerusalem church and half-brother of the Lord. James shows his leadership in the Council of Jerusalem (recorded in *Acts 15*) where, following a dispute between a group of converted Pharisees and the apostles Peter, Paul and Barnabas, James makes a concluding remark quoting from the prophet Amos. God promised, through Amos, to return and rebuild David's fallen tent so that a remnant of men may seek the Lord, together with all the Gentiles who bear God's name (*Acts 15: 16-17; Amos 9: 11-12*). This is at a time when God will bring back the exiles of Israel into the land (*Amos 9: 13-15*).

The Apostle John in Revelation also sees the full measure of Judah and Israel coming into God's kingdom with a symbolic 144,000, or 12,000 from each tribe (*Rev. 7: 1-8*). Clearly the apostles and leaders of the Church saw their mission in terms of reaching out to all the people of Israel in fulfilment of Old Testament prophecy and according to the command of Christ. The Church then became a union of Judah and Israel, and eventually as united Israel it re-settled in Palestine establishing

---

[78] Ibid, pp. 168, 203

communities and building churches in fulfilment of those prophecies.

One possible argument against this might be the question of Paul's teachings, and whether he taught that Judah was to be reunited with the northern tribes of Israel under the Messiah. I think Paul does touch upon this, although it is not so strong in his teachings for a number of reasons. It was Paul who was primarily chosen as an apostle to the Gentiles, to their kings, but also to the sons of Israel (*Acts 9: 15*). Primarily then his ministry was to Gentiles, and his area of responsibility mainly covered regions around the Mediterranean Sea where Jewish traders had settled and were living side by side with the local Gentile population. The Holy Spirit had prevented Paul from entering Asia where many of the scattered Israelites had settled, that was Peter's area of responsibility. Also Paul was not one of the twelve sent out by Jesus to the lost sheep of the house of Israel as the other apostles had been (*Matt. 10*). Thus the question is not so important in Paul's teachings, but I think he does address the question, especially in Romans 9-11, and he does take the gospel to some of the scattered Israelites through his ministry.

The new Israel though is the kingdom of heaven where faith is of importance, not simply birthright or possession of land. This kingdom is to spread through the whole earth as yeast spreads through dough, or a mustard seed produces a tree that grows across the whole garden (*Matt. 13*). The king of this kingdom is the promised Messiah from the line of David, and the domain is the Church that exists across the whole earth where the wheat will grow amongst the weeds until the time of the end. As noted in the prophetic writings, the land of Israel was too small to contain the full promise of God, where the descendants of Abraham were promised to be as numerous as the 'sand on the seashore' and Abraham's blessing was ultimately for all nations across the world. The gospel then extended to the Gentile nations according to the promise to Abraham, and as Isaiah reminded his readers (*Isa. 49: 6*), but the kingdom of God exists as primarily a spiritual kingdom upon the face of the whole earth where entry is by faith in Christ.

It may be argued as well that failure to recognise the place of the northern tribes of Israel, who were taken into exile under the Assyrians, is itself a form of replacement theology. If it is believed that they disappeared for good and were replaced by Judah and Benjamin as representative of Israel, then all the promises to those tribes, especially the birthright promise to Joseph and Ephraim, become null and void. As noted at the start of the previous chapter, Jacob-Israel blessed Joseph, saying that all of his blessings would be upon the head of Joseph and by extension also upon his offspring Ephraim and Manasseh (*Gen 49: 26*). Both Ephraim and Manasseh were promised that they would be called by the name of Abraham, Isaac and Jacob-Israel, and that they would extend across the earth.

Chapter 6

Israel in Matthew's Gospel

In this chapter I will examine the teachings of Jesus, and how the Gospel writers understood Jesus' purpose in terms of the fulfilment of prophecies relating to Israel. The main focus will be on Matthew's Gospel, and comparison with the teachings of the prophets, especially Zechariah. This is though only a brief look at the Gospels and a much more detailed look at the teachings of Jesus is really necessary to do it full justice.

Matthew 1. Jesus' birth

Matthew starts by giving the genealogy of Jesus through the line of Joseph, a son of David, but emphasizes the virgin birth quoting *Isaiah (Isa. 7: 14)*, noting that he will be called Immanuel, meaning 'God with us' (*Matt. 1: 23*). Matthew also records that the angel instructed Joseph to call his son Jesus, the Greek form of Joshua, which means 'to save' because he will save *his people* from their sins (*Matt. 1: 21*). With the coming of the Magi, the chief priests and teachers of the law replied to Herod that the Messianic Judaic ruler was to be born in Bethlehem, and he will be a shepherd to Israel (*Matt. 2: 6; Mic. 5: 2*). However, king Herod wanted to kill the promised Messiah.

Luke offers greater depth in both the events that led to the birth of the prophet John, and the events that led to the birth of Jesus. Mary is recorded as having had a vision of an angel who informed her of the forthcoming birth, and is told that her son Jesus will rule on the throne of David according to God's promise, thus ruling over the house of Jacob forever; that is over both Judah and Israel (*Luke 1: 33*). Mary gives thanks and praise to God and states that Jesus is to be a help to Israel, as God has now remembered to be merciful to Abraham and his

79

descendents according to his promise to the Patriarchs. With the birth of John the Baptist, Zechariah, John's father, offers praise to the God of Israel asserting that a 'horn of salvation' has been raised up in the house of David, thus remembering the covenant of promise to Abraham, and that John would be a prophet preparing the way for the Lord (*Luke 1: 67-72, 76*). Later, when Jesus was presented to the temple, Simeon, who had been promised by God that he would see the coming Messiah who would be the 'consolation of Israel', spoke up and prophesied that Jesus would be a light to the Gentiles, and will bring glory to the people of Israel. God's salvation would be revealed to all people (*Luke 2: 25-32*). But he warned Mary and Joseph that the child would cause some to fall, and some to rise in Israel with the thoughts of many hearts exposed (*Luke 2: 34-35*). Anna, the prophetess from the Israelite tribe of Asher, also spoke about Jesus to all she met in the temple area.

Matthew 10. Shepherding the Lost Sheep of Israel

As noted already in the previous chapter, in *Matthew 10* Jesus is recorded as sending out the twelve disciples to preach abroad the kingdom of God as they were commanded to go to the 'lost sheep of the house of Israel' (*Matt. 10: 6*), a reference to biblical prophecy that God would be a faithful shepherd to the exiled people of Israel (especially *Ezek. 34: 1-12* and *Jer. 50: 4-6*). In these passages then God himself promised to be a shepherd to the scattered lost sheep of the house of Israel, prophecies that Jesus fulfilled.

Matthew 13. Kingdom Parables

Jesus also had much to say about the 'kingdom of Heaven' or the 'kingdom of God,' especially in his many parables (See for instance *Matt. 13*). The Pharisees and teachers of the law saw the nation of Israel ideally as a single kingdom within a particular land with one king, but Jesus taught that the new kingdom of God was to have a different structure, commenting that the new kingdom would be different to that which had gone before. Jesus was to be the eternal Messianic king from David's line. Zion was to have a new name (from *Isa. 62: 1-2*) and many of Jesus' parables need to be read in light of Old Testament prophecies, and in the context of the situation of first century Judea.

In these parables, Jesus said that the wheat and weeds would grow up together in the world and only be separated at the end of the age so that the good crop would not be damaged (*Matt. 13: 24-30*). No longer would there be a single nation in a single land, an entity that the religious Jews were looking for, instead the new kingdom would be scattered amongst the nations.

The kingdom of heaven was also compared to a mustard seed, in that although it is the smallest of garden seeds, it grows into the largest garden tree, spreading beyond its borders, but in doing so it allowed the birds of the air to sheltered and perch on its branches.[79] Incidentally, Joseph's blessing was that his line would spread over a wall and outside of their borders. Also Jesus said that the kingdom of heaven is like yeast that spreads through the whole dough (*Matt. 13: 31-33*). In these parables Jesus was saying that the kingdom of heaven would be in the whole world, and not limited to a single state, as had been the case in the past. This kingdom would then spread throughout the world and transform it according to God's government of peace. Merchants would see such great value in the new kingdom that they would be willing to sell all they had in order to enter in. Jesus was not thinking then of setting up a single nation in a single land, but one spread across the whole earth in fulfilment

---

[79] The mustard tree caused problems for the Pharisees and teachers of the law because it spread outside of clearly marked borders, thus breaking the Mosaic Law. Because it became a tree its fruit could not be harvested until the fifth year, but its life span was only a few years and the tree might then have died before its fruit could be used (see *Lev. 19: 19, 23*).

of the promise given to Abraham, that his descendants would be a blessing to all nations on earth. However, Jesus also told his disciples that he spoke in parables so that those with callous hearts would not understand his message (*Matt. 13: 10-15*).

Matthew 21. Jerusalem and the Fig Tree

In this chapter, Matthew records the triumphal entry into Jerusalem by Jesus, who chose to ride on a colt, the foal of a donkey (*Matt. 21: 1-6*). In doing this Jesus was fulfilling the prophecy of *Zech. 9: 9* as a sign of the king, coming in deliberate humility and gentleness, as a message to the offspring of Zion. Jesus then identified himself with the prophecies of Zechariah. As noted, Zechariah prophesied reunion between Judah and Israel, but also God warned of further division for those in rebellion against him. As Jesus entered Jerusalem the people cried out the Messianic greetings, 'Hosanna to the Son of David' and 'Blessed is he who comes in the name of the Lord' (*Matt. 21: 9*). Jesus then entered the temple area and cleared it of the corrupt money changers, but also he spent time healing those who came to him (*Matt. 21: 12-14*).

Jesus later performed a symbolic act by cursing a fig tree that was not bearing fruit, but only lovely green leaves (*Matt. 21: 18-22 & Mark 11: 12-21*). Jesus did this because the fig tree had no fruit, even though it was not the season for figs; commenting further that it would never bear fruit again. This took place shortly after Jesus had cleared the temple, accusing the religious authorities of turning the temple into a den of robbers (with reference to *Jer. 7: 11*), thus the cursed fig tree should be seen as a reference to the old covenant temple authorities and system of worship. The prophet Micah commented that God would be unhappy when, at harvest time, he couldn't find any of the grapes or 'early figs' that he desired, noting the wickedness of the people (*Mic. 7: 1-7*). There also appears to be a symbolic reference in this act to *Jeremiah 24* (*Jer. 24: 1-10*) where the prophet sees God placing two baskets of figs, one good and one bad, in front of the temple. According to Jeremiah, the figs represented the division of Judah into a basket that was bearing fruit according to God's righteousness, and those who were not. God's promise to the basket of good figs was to give them a heart to seek after him, while the basket of bad fruit would receive nothing. In other words the only way the Jewish nation could bear fruit in the future was through their Messiah as the old system of worship and temple authority had been totally replaced by the new sacrifice of Christ. It may be seen then that the intention of Jesus was to separate out the 'good figs' of the tribe of Judah from the 'bad figs.'

Jesus went on to say that the kingdom of God would be taken away from the chief priests and Pharisees and given to those who would produce the fruit of the kingdom. In a parable Jesus said that even though they knew he was the heir of the vineyard, they planned to kill him anyway along with the servants the prophets who had gone before, and therefore they planned to steal the inheritance from the Son (*Matt. 21: 33-42*). Although the Judaic chief priests and Pharisees were condemned by Jesus and told that they would lose their position, the first Christians were almost entirely Jewish. In other words a remnant as one third of Judah remained and continued according to God's promise while it was the rebellious two thirds that were to be cut off (*Zech. 13: 7-9*). Although the Church gradually lost its Jewish identity as more and more Gentiles joined, the Church may be seen as a legitimate continuation of part of the tribe Judah today with Jesus as the Messiah seated on David's throne.

Matthew 23. A Desolate House

In Matthew 23 Jesus spoke seven woes over the Pharisees and teachers of the Law, which I think is significant in light of the seven fold blessing of Abraham. In other words, in this declaration Jesus was revoking his covenant of Favour and Union with them according to Zechariah 11. Jesus concluded his statement by commenting that the sins of their forefathers would come upon their generation, all the way from the guilt of the shed blood of Abel to Zechariah the priest who was murdered in the temple. Jesus further commented that their house will be left to them desolate (*Matt. 23: 1-38*), then commenting; 'For I tell you, you will not see me again until you say, 'Blessed is he who comes in the name of the Lord.'' (*Matt. 23: 39*) In Hebrew this last statement is *Baruch ha ba be shem adonai*, a greeting recognised by Jews as being Messianic. This was the greeting the people shouted when Jesus entered Jerusalem on the young donkey. In other words, Jesus was saying to the Pharisees and teachers of the Law that he was the Messiah, and that there would be no one else; as such the only way to find the Messiah was to recognise and accept him. The old ways of temple sacrifice were then brought to nothing, and their 'house' was to suffer desolation. However, even in this harsh judgement there was, and is, mercy to the remnant of Jews, in that a way back to God is still open through Jesus for those who repent and turn to him.

The apostle John also records Jesus' criticisms of the Pharisees where he accuses them of being children of the devil because of their lies and desire to murder him (*John 8: 42-47*). In Revelation, John further noted the words of Jesus, who said that there are some Jews who are not, but are really the synagogue of Satan (*Rev. 2: 9*).

In Matthew's Gospel Jesus' also warned his followers to beware of the leaven, or yeast, of the Pharisees and Sadducees (*Matt. 16: 6*). Were these comments overly rhetorical and just figures of speech on the part of Jesus? Most Christians ignore the significance of what is said in the passage viewing the Pharisees as mere legalistic religious ideologues. However, there is evidence to suggest that the Pharisees had already embraced, or been influenced by, pagan political philosophy, working it into their own theology. By the third century BC, Jewish philosophers such as Artapanus and Aristobulus were already sympathetic to the works of Plato believing that Moses had taught Orpheus, and Aristobulus believed further that the writing of Moses had heavily influenced both Plato and Pythagoras. However, both Plato and Pythagoras may have been involved in the esotericism of Egyptian and Babylonian paganism. Plato also influenced Philo, and the unconverted Saul, who was a rising and zealous star in the Sanhedrin, had been trained in Greek philosophy as well as studying under Gamaliel. In other words, in first century Palestine the beliefs of the Greek thinkers, and therefore also perhaps that of Babylon and Egypt, had some influence upon the leadership of the Jewish state, more especially through the political beliefs of the Pharisees and ruling classes. This may be seen when it is considered in light of the political philosophy of Plato. I am suggesting that the class divisions of Plato's *Republic* were also evident in the practices of the Pharisees in the first century setting who were acting like Plato's 'philosopher kings'. The majority of Jews though were forced into an impoverished and subservient position through exploitation. In the *Republic*, Plato had set out his social order for the ideal city-state of *Polis* with a subservient population ruled over by philosopher kings and a high class military.

Jesus criticised the Pharisees commenting that they should not be called 'Rabbis' because they were 'brothers' with their fellow Jews (*Matt. 23: 8*). He therefore condemned them for their exploitation of the poor, an exploitation that was incidentally allowable in their Mosaic interpretation, the 'Tradition of the Elders,' but not in the Torah. Jesus also commented that the Pharisees and teachers of the Law would fill up on the sins of their forefathers (sins that included murder and idolatry in the Old Testament history) even as their house would be left to them desolate (*Matt. 23: 32*).

Interestingly, in Revelation John sees a harlot riding the beast and the woman is identified as Mystery Babylon, a great city (Gk polis) who rules over the earth (*Rev. 17: 5, 18*), but the woman will eventually be brought to nothing, and her destruction will come in one hour (*Rev. 18*). In other words, Jesus' was harsh towards the Pharisees and teachers of the Law because he could see beyond the surface and see their hearts as they were perhaps beginning to embrace the politics of Mystery Babylon in their class-ridden politics. They were indeed being seduced and blinded by their privileged position, unable to see the Messiah and understand the full counsel of Old Testament teachings. However, it is important to stress that these prophesies were not given against all Jews, but against a corrupt and idolatrous leadership who were exploiting the poor in Jewish society. The poor of Jewish society were very much the victims of this type of political philosophy.

Matthew 24. End Time Prophecies

In Matthew 24 Jesus speaks prophesies about events to come. Firstly, he comments that the temple will be levelled with no stone left unturned (*Matt. 24: 2*). This was fulfilled in AD 68-70 when the Roman armies brought judgement against Jerusalem, destroying the temple and leaving no stone unturned in order to extract the gold. There are though I think two prophecies interwoven into this passage. One concerns the judgement against Judah in the first century BC; the second concerns the second coming of Jesus. The sign of the first judgement is the 'abomination that causes desolation' which was a sign for the Christians to flee to the hills and therefore escape the judgement that was to come upon Jerusalem (*Matt. 24: 15-22*). Eusebius[80] has a lot to say about this judgement upon Jerusalem in his *Ecclesiastical History*, and how the Christians escaped because of Jesus' prophecy, although a complete discussion of this will take us away from the theme of the book.

The sign of the second judgement is the sign of the fig tree producing more green leaves (*Matt. 24: 32-33*). While Jesus cursed the fig tree, he said that it will again appear bringing

---

[80] Cruse, C.F. (trans.), *The Ecclesiastical History of Eusebius Pamphilus - Bishop of Caesarea, In Palestine*, 1850. Reprinted as *Eusebius' Ecclesiastical History*, Baker Book House, 1995.

forth more green leaves in the future, noting that this will be a sign of the end of the age (*Matt. 24: 32 & Mark 13: 28*). Some Christian Zionists use this statement about the fig tree sprouting more green leaves in order to legitimise the modern State of Israel, but totally miss the point about the green leaves. Hal Lindsey for instance comments that this is an important sign of the restoration of the Jews to the land.[81] However, green leaves speak of outward glory, but no inner fruit. Jesus was looking for the inner fruit not the outward show. Therefore as a symbolic act Jesus cursed the tree *because* it was only bearing green leaves, and not fruit. The fruitless fig tree was thus representative of the Jewish ruling authorities and their lack of fruit. I believe that Jesus' comments should be understood to mean that a nation called Israel will return bearing more green leaves, i.e. having the external appearance of Israel, but not bearing the required fruit. The prophecy of Jesus then may be interpreted to imply that a separate Jewish nation would arise again in the future bearing more green leaves before the end of the age, but lacking the fruit that God requires, thus having no part in the true Israel that is a union of Jews, Israelites and Gentiles in the Church.

The re-emergence of such a state of Israel then may be seen as a sign that the second coming is near. God has allowed the State of Israel to exist as part of his permissive will; that is he has permitted Israel to exist as a nation, but Israel is not living according to God's directive will, which is to bear fruit according to God's righteousness. Indeed it is impossible for the State of Israel to bring forth the fruit that God requires outside of Christ; instead the Church is the true Israel of God.

Throughout Matthew's Gospel he highlights how Jesus fulfilled the Old Testament prophecies that spoke of the coming Messiah. Jesus was to be the Messianic king from David's line, the Saviour for his people, and a shepherd to the lost people of the house of Israel. Jesus came to unite Judah and Israel, but he

---

[81] Lindsay, H, *The Late Great Planet Earth*, London: Lakeland / Zondervan, 1970, p. 53

also condemned the faithless leaders, the chief priests and Pharisees who had corrupted God's people with exploitation and false teaching. Jesus then broke his covenant of Union and Favour with that two-thirds part of Judaism according to Zechariah's prophecy by pronouncing that their house would be left to them desolate. However, God remembered his promise to Abraham by making a new covenant with those Jews who followed him and who heard his voice. The remnant of Judah was promised restoration under the Messiah, a promise that continues to this day. The next chapter will look at the New Testament letters of Paul to see how the early Church saw its position before God.

Chapter 7

New Testament Letters

In this chapter it will be interesting to look at the writings of the New Testament apostles and their teachings, especially Paul's writing and influence. What is clear is that Paul was presenting a message that he asserted came by revelation, and as part of this message he worked to build unity between Gentile and Jewish converts because both were being built together into God's temple, which is the body of Christ.

Letter to the Romans

The letter to the Roman Christians was probably written sometime around AD 57. The Church in Rome at the time consisted of Gentile and Jewish believers, and Paul was partly writing to encourage greater unity. There was seemingly some separation between the Gentiles, who expressed their freedom in Christ, and Jewish believers who were following certain of the Old Testament practices. Unlike other churches where Jewish believers were in a majority, in Rome the Gentiles formed the larger grouping and there was some distrust between the two sides. Paul also set out his gospel and theology to a church that was living in the heart of the pagan world with its corruption and idolatry. Part of Paul's thinking then was to build and encourage Christian unity in the pagan city by explaining God's universal plan of salvation and righteousness that was to include Jews and Gentiles.

The main passage from Romans that Christian Zionists appeal to in support of their interpretation of theology is the passage in *Romans 9, 10 and 11* where the Jews are said to be the 'elect' of God. These three chapters need to be taken as a single discussion, (and in context with all of Paul's teaching, especially in Romans) and Paul does mention that an 'elect' of

89

Jews have received grace (*Rom. 9: 11; Rom. 11: 7; Rom. 11: 28*). The question of God's election in general is though problematic with various opinions voiced, although questions about predestination and freewill, and the five points of Calvinism are, thankfully, beyond the scope of this present study. But it may be asked, in what sense does Paul say the Jews are the 'elect' of God? Paul notes (*Rom. 9: 6*) that 'not all who are descended from Israel are Israel,' but only those born according to the promise of God (*Rom. 9: 7-9*). As an example of this type of election Paul uses the birth of Jacob and Esau where the younger brother, Jacob, was called forward for God's express purposes. Election in the context here is concerned with God's divine global plan of salvation for mankind. Paul (*Rom. 9: 25-27*) notes that God will call a people who are not (yet) his people (*Hosea 1: 10; and 2: 23*), and that only a remnant of Israel will be saved (*Isa. 10: 20-25; Isa. 11: 12-16*).

Paul notes that there is now no difference between Jew and Gentile in terms of their status before God, both must come to Christ to receive righteousness the same way; that is through faith (*Rom. 10: 11-13*). Paul also notes that God will justify both the Jews and the Gentiles through the same faith, and that righteousness from God has come to all that is apart from the Mosaic Law, but nevertheless attested to by the prophets and the Law (*Rom. 3: 21-31*).

In terms of an election of a remnant of Israel being saved, Paul mentions (*Rom. 11: 4*) that in the time of Elijah, God kept seven thousand Israelites who had not bowed the knee to Baal. Paul comments (*Rom. 11: 5*) that '...at the present time there is a remnant chosen by grace', but Paul also notes (*Rom. 11: 7*) that 'the others were hardened' a reference to those Jews who had rejected Jesus in the time of Paul's writing (see *Isa. 29: 10*). In *Romans 11* Paul asserts that the unbelieving Jews had been cut out of the olive tree with the Gentiles grafted in. But this was not to make the Gentiles proud, but instead they should be humble and thankful and work for the restoration of the unbelieving Jews who may be grafted in again if they accept

Christ. Gentile Christians are further called to make the Jews envious of their new faith through their faithfulness, love and good conduct (*Rom. 11: 11*). As noted, in the Old Testament Zechariah sees the good shepherd, the 'man who is close to [the Lord]', struck with the sword so that the sheep will be scattered (*Zech. 13: 7*). As a result of this two thirds of the sheep will be cut off, while the other one third will be tested and refined in the fire as silver or gold. This remnant will then call on the Lord and become God's people (*Zech. 13: 9*).

One aspect of the theology of some Christian Zionists that causes problems is that it develops a dualistic theology with two olive trees, or two streams of grace; one dispensation for the Jews and one for Gentiles, but Paul only saw one olive root for both Jew and Gentile in *Romans 11*. The great hope of Paul was that in the end all Israel will be saved by being re-grafted into the single olive tree as returning natural branches (*Rom. 11: 23*), once the full measure of Gentiles had been grafted in. Paul (*Rom. 11: 28*) mentions that Israel is loved on account of the Patriarchs because of God's 'election' and will be saved as a people in the end as a result of God's promise to Abraham; although Paul uses the present tense (*Rom. 11: 31*) to argue that they may *now* receive mercy on account of the Patriarchs. This statement, and Paul's references to Hosea, I believe should be interpreted as meaning that Paul looked forward to the conversion of the scattered northern Israelites, as well as the eventual conversion of remaining Jews, as the gospel was spreading across the world. Paul's reference to all Israel must include the northern tribes as well as Judah and Benjamin.

Paul also commented earlier in the letter that Abraham's faith was credited to him as righteousness before his circumcision, and therefore he is the father of the uncircumcised as well as the circumcised, and the promise of Abraham was that he would be a forefather of the whole world, a promise that was to come through faith (*Rom. 4: 1-25*). The use of the word 'election' (*Rom 9-11*) doesn't mean that the Jews can still be reconciled to God under the old covenant, but instead the passage is perhaps a reference to an end time revival of Jews. This would mean then that they are to receive grace and mercy to believe in the work of Christ in the end. Under this scenario they will finally come to place their faith in Christ because of grace given on account of the promise made to the Patriarchs, but as Paul notes the gospel message *now* goes to Jews everywhere and the door to Christ is open to all. 'Election' was and is to do with God's global plan of salvation; first a remnant of faithful Jews and Israelites would be saved at the foundation of the Church, then the full measure of Gentiles would be brought in, then the remaining Jews towards the end. Completion of God's 'election' will be achieved when the remaining Jews accept Christ, and it will mean 'life from the dead' for all when God's plan of salvation is complete (*Rom. 11: 15*). The action of Christians today then should not be to seek to absolve Jews of their responsibility and need for the Messiah by proposing two streams of grace, but instead to love the Jews enough to bring them to the Messiah, back into their own natural olive tree. This olive tree is today identifiable as the Christian community consisting of Jews, Gentiles and Israelites grafted together into the Israelite olive root. While I believe and pray that God will bring the remaining Jews to faith in Christ in the end in this way, I do not believe that political or religious Zionism, which is outside of Christ, has any place in God's plan. The Jews today do not need to enter Palestine to receive God's mercy and grace; it is available across the whole world, but only through Christ.

Letter to the Galatians

Paul wrote the letter to the Galatians to counter certain Jewish Christians who were seeking to impose Jewish practices upon the believers in that area. There is uncertainty though over the exact timing of the letter, with various dates given between AD 48-57, and whether it was written to believers in the northern or southern regions of Galatia. Perhaps Paul had believers from both regions in mind. Later the letter was considered an important document of the Protestant Reformation where salvation was accepted as being by faith alone, and thus challenging the theology of the Roman Catholic Church that then required faith and works of indulgences. However, Paul was writing to challenge the re-imposition of Mosaic legal requirements upon the new believers by some Jewish converts.

In this letter, Paul effectively challenged those converts from Judaism who were seeking to re-introduce aspects of the Mosaic Law to the Christians in Galatia, both to Jews and Gentiles. Paul accused such legalists of confusing and corrupting the gospel of grace (*Gal. 1: 7*), a gospel that Paul himself had previously preached to the Galatians. But this wasn't just a problem for the Galatians'; it was part of a crisis for the growing Christian community as a whole. Paul asserted that his gospel had not come through men, but was given to him as a revelation from God, although Paul had submitted his message to the Jerusalem leaders, and they had supported it and his work amongst the Gentiles. But a situation had later arisen in Jerusalem (*Gal. 2*) where the leaders of the Church started to impose certain Jewish practices upon Gentile converts, and even Peter and Barnabas were compromised in this. However, Paul opposed them because of his commitment to the work of Jesus Christ as being sufficient for justification before God, a work that is to be received by faith. No one, Paul noted, could be justified before God by observing the Law, or by working out one's own salvation, but it could only be through faith in Jesus Christ.

Paul asked his readers (*Gal. 3: 6*) to consider Abraham as the father of those who believe, because Abraham had believed God and that faith was credited to him as righteousness. Therefore those who have put their trust in Christ have become children of Abraham, and this includes both Jews and Gentiles. The promise to Abraham was that 'All nations will be blessed through you,' (*Gal. 3: 8*) and through faith the blessing given to Abraham has come upon the Gentile believers

(*Gal. 3: 9, 14*). However, in contrast those who rely on the Law of Moses for salvation are in fact under a curse, because according to Scripture those who do not completely fulfil the law are cursed (*Gal. 3: 10; Deut. 27: 26*). Thankfully, Christ has now redeemed those who have faith in him from the curse of the Law by becoming a curse for us, because he was hung on a tree according to biblical prophecy (*Gal. 3: 13*).

Paul further notes that Christ came to fulfil the promise given to Abraham because Jesus Christ is the 'seed' of Abraham (*Gal. 3: 16*). The everlasting covenant that God made with Abraham was confirmed *in flesh*. Significant theology that is spiritual in nature is often revealed in Scripture through material events and people, thus having both a material and a spiritual application. But while there are dual aspects, Judeo-Christian theology rejects dualistic theology, because the spiritual and material are being brought together in Christ. Although Abraham's children of the flesh, especially Ephraim and Manasseh's line, grew in number as promised into the nations of Israel, the true Israel of the everlasting covenant could only be formed in a spiritual sense in the body of Jesus Christ, who was the promised spiritual 'seed' of Abraham, but a seed born in the flesh. Thus the true Israel is the spiritual Church that is being built up together into the heavenly tabernacle, which is Christ's own body. This is the reason why all, whether Jew, Israelite or Gentile must come to Christ in the same way to receive the fullness of Israel. It is not replacement theology because all must come in through the same door; instead it is about unity, continuity and fulfilment with God's promises to Abraham.

But while the world was waiting for Christ, the Law of Moses was given because of transgression until the promise of the seed, that is Jesus Christ, came (*Gal. 3: 19*). Paul notes that the Law of Moses could not, and did not, set aside the covenant previously given to Abraham because Abraham's covenant was given as a promise from God as an inheritance to both Jews and Gentiles (*Gal. 3: 17-18*). The Mosaic Law had been given with Moses acting as a mediator between Israel and God. Thus, those who seek to impose the Law of Moses *today*, because they consider it to be God's covenant, overlook the greater covenant that God had first promised to Abraham *that is now to be received by faith* by all, and could never be replaced by a separate mediated legal code.[82]

Through Christ, the promise of God has now set Christians free from bondage to the Law because it is a greater covenant than the Law of Moses. Paul commented that the Law of Moses was an interim measure meant to eventually lead people to Christ when the time of Christ finally came (*Gal. 3: 21-24*). Neither under this new covenant is there now any difference in this regard between Jew or Greek, male or female, slave or free, because all who are in Christ are children of God irrespective of their nationality, gender or social status; and all of this is the free gift of God, given to set free those who accept Christ's gift of grace (*Gal. 3: 26-29*).

Paul further urges his readers not to seek after the old city of Jerusalem with its system of worship because it is not the city of the promise. Instead, our new city of Jerusalem is free and above. According to Paul, Abraham had two sons, one by the free woman Sarah, and the other son by the slave woman Hagar. The son of the free woman was given as a result of the promise of God. The two women then also represent two covenants; the covenant of the slave woman, Hagar, represents Mount Sinai in Arabia and her children are in slavery under the Mosaic Law. Paul notes that Hagar also represents the old city of Jerusalem, whereas Sarah represents the New Jerusalem that is above and free (*Gal. 4: 21-26*). As such, all, both Jew and Gentile, are urged to have nothing to do with the slavery that comes by the Law, but are instead urged to enter into the inheritance of the free woman and her promised son Isaac (*Gal. 4: 28-31*).

---

[82] In fact it has always been by faith and Abraham is the father of faith because he believed God and it was accredited to him as righteousness

Letter to the Ephesians

The letter to the Ephesians was written partly to explain the unity that God has planned between Jews and Gentiles, and also to reveal the extent of God's grace in Christ. In the letter, Paul elaborates on the gospel, whereby God's desire is to bring everything to unity and fullness in Christ. He comments that God seeks to 'bring all things in heaven and on earth together under one head, even Christ' (*Eph. 1: 10*). Paul asserts that Christ has been raised from the dead and now seated in heavenly places where he has been given the highest authority and accolade. Now God is bringing everything under his feet, as Christ has been appointed the 'head over everything for the church, which is his body, and the fullness of him who fills everything in every way' (*Eph. 1: 20-23*). Christian believers, both Jews and Gentiles, have also now been raised up with Christ and made alive in him (*Eph. 2: 4-6*).

Paul further expands on the message of unity asserting that the Gentiles have now been brought close to God alongside the Jews. Although Gentiles were once considered 'foreigners to the covenants of promise' and 'excluded from citizenship in Israel' they have now been brought near through the blood of Christ (*Eph. 2: 11-13*). The two have been made one and the 'dividing wall of hostility' has been removed between the Israelites and Gentiles as God has now destroyed the legal barriers in his own flesh. It was God's purpose to make one new man out of the two, thus bringing peace and unity to both communities (*Eph. 2: 14-16*). Further to this, God has made Gentile believers 'fellow-citizens with God's people' and equal members of 'God's household;' therefore Gentiles can no longer be considered 'foreigners and aliens' to the Jews. God's household is further being built into a holy temple where the prophets and apostles have provided foundations with Christ as the chief cornerstone. This holy temple, the Church, which is Christ's body, is rising up and being built together in unity, a unity that consists of both Jews and Gentiles, into a dwelling place for God's Spirit (*Eph. 2: 19-22*).

Paul also asserts that this message had previously been hidden from previous generations, but that now God has chosen to reveal this mystery through Paul; a message that reveals that God's intention is that Gentiles are heirs with Israel, 'members together of one body' and sharing in the promises of God in Jesus Christ (*Eph. 3: 1-6*).

Letter to the Hebrews

There would appear to be some uncertainty over the authorship of the letter to the Hebrews, and it is generally considered today that it was not the Apostle Paul, although for a good deal of Church history the letter was attributed to Paul. Eusebius suggested though that the letter to the Hebrews was written by Paul in Hebrew, and translated into Greek by either Luke or Clement, which would explain the non-Pauline phraseology.[83] There is though no mention in the letter itself of the author's name, but it would seem that it was someone at least close to Paul because the theology contained in the letter covers many of the same themes as Paul's teachings, and it expresses concern for Timothy, Paul's beloved co-worker in the closing comments. In fact the theology of Hebrews is to some extent an extension of the arguments presented in the letters to the Galatians and Ephesians relating to the temple and to Abraham and Isaac, and also in terms of the place of the Jews within the new covenant. The writer implores Jewish converts not to turn back to their old practices in Judaism. The content of Hebrews then contains a message that is very close to Paul's teaching, a message that Paul said was given to him by

---

[83] Cruse, C.F. (trans.), *The Ecclesiastical History of Eusebius Pamphilus -*, Op. cit., Book III, Chapter XXXVIII, 1850. Reprinted as *Eusebius' Ecclesiastical History*, Baker Book House, (1995), p. 124

revelation from God. If it wasn't Paul it was someone very close to him.

Another possible candidate for authorship of Hebrews who has been mentioned in historical texts is Barnabas. Tertullian, writing in *De Pudicitia* around AD 200, mentioned an Epistle to the Hebrews written by Barnabas. Barnabas would certainly fit the bill; he was from the Levitical line and was a close companion of Paul as both shared in ministry, even travelling together for a while; that is until the dispute over Mark's departure caused a temporary parting of the ways. Mark was a nephew of Barnabas, but later Paul is reconciled to Mark, and asks for him to come to him in prison, commenting on his usefulness to him (*2 Tim. 4: 11*). This position in the early Church, and lineage with the Levitical priestly line, would have given Barnabas sufficient weight amongst his hearers, especially those Jewish converts from the priesthood. He would therefore have been a suitable candidate for writing such a letter, as the purpose was to encourage Jewish believers to remain with the Christian faith and not revert back to their former legalistic practices of worship in times of trouble. However, the question of authorship remains unresolved, and Paul may indeed have written it in the way Eusebius asserts.

In a number of places in the letter the writer calls readers to persevere and not turn back to the old ways in Judaism that had now been superseded by Christ's work on the cross. The letter was written to the Hebrews of the first century Church, but the subject matter is still relevant to us today. The central theme of the letter is the person of Jesus Christ; who he is, and what he has done in fulfilment of Old Testament writings and prophecies, especially as the new Church relates to the fulfilment of temple worship and practice.

At the start of the letter Christ is presented as the co-worker with the Father in the Creation, and therefore he is higher than the angels, as the Son of God, and the exact representation of the Father, sustaining all things by his powerful word (*Heb. 1: 1-14*). Next we see Christ as the son of man, but noting also that everything is subject to him. In this position, as both God and man, Christ made the perfect sacrifice for sin for all time, with the purpose of bringing many men and women to the same glory that Christ now has. As the argument of Hebrews develops it becomes clear that the glorification of the new temple, that is the Church, is of central importance to the writer's thinking. In order to bring glory to the new temple it was thus necessary for Christ to become fully human so that he could set people free from the bondage to sin. In doing this Christ was acting as the perfect high priest, enabling redemption for all.

In the next chapter the writer to the Hebrews assert that Jesus was greater than Moses, and that Jesus is a high priest appointed over the house of God, and that the Church itself is now that house of God (*Heb. 3: 6*). The converted Jews were further exhorted not to harden their hearts and turn back as they had now heard the message of the gospel. In this exhortation they were urged not to be like the Israelites who had heard God in the desert and then wanted to go back to Egypt (*Heb. 3: 7-11; Ps. 95: 7-11*).

Jesus is further presented in Hebrews as the great high priest, not of the order of Aaron, but of the order of Melchizedek. God made an oath by his own name to Abraham, promising to bless him and give him many descendants. While the Law was given through Moses, who was acting as the mediator, the oath that God gave to Abraham was by his own name and therefore greater. Under this blessing Abraham gave a tenth of the plunder to Melchizedek the priest, thus showing that Melchizedek was a greater priest than Levi because Levi was a descendent of Abraham (*Heb. 6: 9*). Whereas the sacrifices of Levi were incomplete the new covenant of Christ was perfect and the former one given to Moses has therefore been 'set aside' (*Heb. 7: 18*). The true tabernacle then is not a building, or a tent, made by human hands, but is now one made by God (*Heb. 8: 2*), and thus Jesus' ministry is far superior to that of Moses.

The writer to the Hebrews also appeals to the writing of Jeremiah to make the point that God has promised a new covenant to the people of Israel (*Heb. 8: 8-12; Jer. 31: 31-34*).

"The time is coming," declares the LORD, "when I will make a new covenant with the house of Israel and with the house of Judah.

It will not be like the covenant I made with their forefathers when I took them by the hand to lead them out of Egypt, because they broke my covenant, though I was a husband to them," declares the LORD.

"This is the covenant I will make with the house of Israel after that time," declares the LORD. "I will put my law in their minds and write it on their hearts. I will be their God, and they will be my people.

No longer will a man teach his neighbour, or a man his brother, saying, 'Know the LORD,' because they will all know me, from the least of them to the greatest," declares the LORD. "For I will forgive their wickedness and will remember their sins no more."

Because the sacrifice of Jesus is so much better than the requirements of the Mosaic Law, then the new covenant that Jesus established has made the old Mosaic one 'obsolete' (*Heb. 8: 13*). The tabernacle, that is Jesus, is perfect, and he took his own blood in and made a perfect sacrifice (*Heb. 9: 11-12*) making perfect forever those who are being made holy. The new covenant promise has thus made Christians heirs of an eternal inheritance (*Heb. 9: 15*), and the Law of Moses was merely a shadow of the greater things that were to come (*Heb. 10: 1*).

Importantly, the letter to the Hebrews comments that Jesus provided everything for the establishment of the new covenant, and all of this was according to the promise freely given to Abraham. Jesus provided the perfect sacrifice with his own blood and has become the great high priest ministering in the heavenly tabernacle, which is his own body, the Church.

Zion's New Name

The writer to the Hebrews also asserts that God's plan was much more than merely bringing a single nation into a particular land, but that it was always about extending blessing to all nations on earth under a heavenly kingdom according to God's promise through Abraham's seed. Many of the Patriarchs received promises that they did not see fulfilled in their own time. They believed them by faith, but their hope was for a heavenly kingdom being 'aliens and strangers' while living on the earth (*Heb. 11: 13*). Abraham went to the Promised Land in faithful obedience to God, but lived in a tent like a stranger in a foreign land, as did Isaac and Jacob (*Heb. 11: 8-10*). But Abraham 'was looking forward to the city with foundations, whose architect and builder is God' (*Heb. 11: 10*) and to a 'better country – a heavenly one' (*Heb. 11: 16*). Instead the promise to Israel is that we, (Jews, Israelites and Gentiles in Christ) have come 'to Mount Zion, to the heavenly Jerusalem, the city of the living God' (*Heb. 12: 22*) and that this city cannot be shaken as an earthly city can (*Heb. 12: 27-28*).

This letter is particularly pertinent to those Christians and Jews who are now placing their hope and faith in the re-establishment of a worldly State of Israel with earthly blessings and an earthly city of Jerusalem with the re-instatement of temple worship. This earthly city is though ruled over by men and women who are in opposition to the message of Christ. Those of faith should instead follow the example of the Patriarch Abraham and place their trust in Christ and look forward to the complete fulfilment of his kingdom rule on earth from the New Jerusalem. The message of Hebrews is that Christ has done everything in providing the sacrifice, the priesthood, and the temple, which is the Church, the body of Christ. From this it may be seen then that the New Israel, the New Jerusalem that is now identifiable as the Church is also being built up in unity in the body of Christ. The glory of God now resides in the tabernacle, which is the Church, and it is God's desire that his ancient people of Israel and Judah should be brought back into this fullness. But the desire of some Christian Zionists to rebuild an earthly temple in Jerusalem is in effect robbing Jews of their full promises in Christ. Instead the rule of Christ has already begun, although it will not be complete until he returns. God, through the biblical writers, promised a New Heaven and a New Earth ruled from the New Jerusalem under the authority of Christ.

Chapter 8

Declaration of Zionist Congress

So far then we have looked at replacement theology as characterised by opponents and its deficiencies together with a detailed study of the rise of Christian Zionism and what it entails. Following this we have examined the Old Testament prophets and the New Testament Gospels, the teachings of Paul in Romans, Galatians, Ephesians, and Hebrews in the context of the historical setting in order to get a better picture of what the Bible really teaches about this subject. We can now return to the question of Zionism and looking in more detail at each of the points from the Declaration of the Third International Christian Zionist Congress held in Jerusalem in February 1996 to consider how they tie up with biblical teaching. For the sake of argument it is assumed that these five points encapsulate the teachings of mainstream Christian Zionism, although there are in reality many different views.

Statement 1 – Elect of God

'God the Father, Almighty, chose the ancient nation and people of Israel, the descendants of Abraham, Isaac and Jacob, to reveal His plan of redemption for the world. They remain elect of God, and without the Jewish nation His redemptive purposes for the world will not be completed.'

The first part of this statement is not very controversial, although it was God's plan to bring forth the Messiah through the tribe of Judah. God's promise to Judah was that the sceptre would not depart from his line until the one to whom tribute belonged was revealed (*Gen. 49: 8-12*). Therefore God chose the lineage of Judah for the purpose of giving birth to Jesus, the

103

King of the Jews, who would redeem Judah, Israel and the Gentile world; this through Christ's sacrificial death on the cross. However, as noted the descendents of Abraham included the northern tribes of Israel who went into exile and did not, at face value, return; only the tribes of Judah, Benjamin, and some Levitical priests returned from Babylonian exile. Whereas the ruler was to come through Judah, the birthright, and therefore the nationhood of Israel, was given to Joseph and Ephraim by Jacob-Israel. It is pertinent then to consider, as I have tried to do in previous chapters, what happened to the northern Israelites in exile. As a result of this consideration I believe it is wrong to identify the present Jewish nation as being truly representative of the whole of Israel because it does not possess the birthright that is in Joseph's lineage. Redemption is now found in Christ, and the commission to spread the gospel message is placed within the Christian Church that is now spiritual Israel; a united spiritual nation based on the ethnic Israelite root that includes the twelve tribes together with Gentiles under the Judaic ruler.

The question of God's election for the Jews is more problematic. As noted from the three chapters of *Romans 9-11* Paul asserts that an elect have now received grace as a remnant of Israel according to the promise of God, but that many Jews were hardened because of their rejection of Christ. But in the end the remaining Jews will be given grace to accept Christ once the full measure of Gentiles have been grafted into the olive root, this on account of the promise given to the Patriarchs. However, this doesn't mean that the Jews can approach God through the sacrificial requirements of the Mosaic Law, which have now become obsolete (*Heb. 8: 13*) because of what Christ has done. It is the promise given to Abraham that continues to those who have faith in Christ to both Jews and Gentiles. God's love for the Patriarchs means that God will remember to bring the remaining Jews to Christ in the end, but it doesn't follow that this must be through a separate Jewish nation. I think as well that it is wrong to believe that God's covenantal will is being worked out through the State of Israel that at present does not accept Jesus as the Messiah. Therefore I believe it wrong to support the nationalistic, expansionist policies of that state.

Statement 2 – Return of Christ

'Jesus of Nazareth is the Messiah and has promised to return to Jerusalem, to Israel and to the world.'

This is correct, but once again there is a question mark against the meaning of words. Jesus is indeed the Messiah to Jews and Gentiles and will return to the Mount of Olives for the Church as stated in *Acts 1: 11*. But not all Christian Zionists believe Jesus was offered to Jews as the Messiah when he came to the Holy Land two thousand years ago. There is also a problem here with the identification of Israel and Jerusalem, because Paul tells us not to look back to the old city of Jerusalem with its legal requirements, but to look forward to the New Jerusalem that is above and free according to God's promise. When Christ returns he will rule from this new city, not the old one made by human hands and requiring imperfect sacrifices, nor one consisting of a secular Jewish political government.

Statement 3 – Repentance for anti-Semitism

'It is reprehensible that generations of Jewish peoples have been killed and persecuted in the name of our Lord, and we challenge the Church to repent of any sins of commission or omission against them.'

Indeed, Jews have suffered much through the years at the hands of Christians, and non-Christians, and this is deeply regrettable, not least because Christians have been called to love the Jews and to witness the merciful message of the gospel. Ill-treatment of the Jews has only hindered the gospel message by hardening hearts. Repentance is more than saying sorry, it is a turning around and living in the light of Christ's commands of love. However, the gospel also calls the Jews to turn to Christ in repentance for their wrongdoing, as there is not one person or nation that is without sin (see for instance *Matt 23*). In order to justify the expulsion and persecution of Jews through history, Jews have often been accused of exploiting their position in Gentile nations, but this is largely unjustified even if a few Jews have exploited their hosts in the past. Most Jews have been industrious and worked with good character in their wanderings in the world. However, any attempt to discuss these questions rationally raises fierce accusations of anti-Semitism. It is though true that many ordinary Jews have suffered unjustly at the hands of Christians through history. Suffice it to say here then that God is the judge of all of us, both Jew and Gentile, and he will bring every deed into the open one day. In light of the human tendency towards sin on all sides there is perhaps a need for a mutual acknowledgement of wrong so that divisions can be healed in Christ.

Statement 4 – Rebirth of Israel

> 'The modern ingathering of the Jewish People to Eretz Israel and the rebirth of the nation of Israel are in fulfilment of biblical prophecies, as written in both Old and New Testaments.'

There may be some limited truth in this statement, but what is important to ask is which biblical prophecies are being fulfilled, and how they are being fulfilled. Do Old Testament prophecies really speak of the return of the State of Israel, or do they instead speak of a spiritual entity in the world that in a very real sense is Israel? What is the purpose of the restoration of a nation called Israel in the end-times, and is it possible to say that the current State of Israel is a fulfillment of those prophecies? The main argument in this book is that most prophecies relating to Israel were fulfilled in and through Christ and in his Church.

There are I believe a few remaining prophecies relating to the modern State of Israel, but I don't believe it can be shown that the State of Israel is in reality fulfilling some positive divine purpose at this time in terms of God's directive will. One of the favourite verse used to support the idea that a State of Israel will be re-established in the present time is *Isaiah 49*, (especially *Isa. 49: 21-22*) which says.

> "See, they will come from afar—some from the north, some from the west, some from the region of Aswan." This is what the Sovereign LORD says: "See, I will beckon to the Gentiles, I will lift up my banner to the peoples; they will bring your sons in their arms and carry your daughters on their shoulders."

The text of *Isaiah 49: 1-26* is discussed more fully earlier in this book, but while at face value this passage seems to strongly support the idea of the restoration of a nation called Israel, it needs to be read in conjunction with other prophecies of the Old Testament and the correct historical context. Hosea records that the northern tribes of Israel were to be rejected as God's people; and instead a people who were not God's people would be called 'sons of the living God' (*Hos. 1: 10*). In the next verse the prophet comments that although the northern tribes were to be expelled from the land, one day Judah and Israel would be reunited under an appointed leader (*Hos. 1: 11*). The prophet Jeremiah (*Jer. 31: 35-37*) also writes that only if the sun, moon and stars fail to shine 'will the descendents of Israel ever cease to be a nation' before God; and only if the heavens can be measured or the earth searched out will God reject 'all the descendents of Israel.' But *Jeremiah 31* is concerned with the new covenant made with both the house of Israel (more specifically Ephraim), and the house of Judah (*Jer. 31: 31*). Under this new covenant God will 'put [his] law in their minds and write it on their hearts' (*Jer. 31: 33*). I can see how the passage in *Isaiah 49* might possibly be read as referring to some form of ingathering of the Jews to Israel in the present time, but I don't believe that interpretation is the correct one because Judah does not represent all of Israel. The ingathering of the Israelites according to the Old Testament prophetic writings is later linked with the reunification of Judah and Israel that occurred with the first coming of the Messiah. Although other passages in the New Testament do speak of the salvation of all Israel (*Romans 11: 23*), and Jesus prophesied that one day the fig tree, as representative of Judah, will re-grow sprouting fresh green leaves, but not the fruit that God desires (*Matt. 24: 32 & Mark 13: 28*).

There is also the question of the name Israel, and whether the Jewish state has a right to that name for their nation today. As noted, this is because the birthright of Reuben was passed to the tribe of Joseph and his sons Ephraim and Manasseh (*1 Chron. 5: 1-2*). Although the Jews, who are from the tribe of Judah, represent a part of Israel, the birthright was given to Joseph's line by Jacob-Israel, and the tribes of Joseph's sons in the northern kingdom did not return from exile en-masse outside of their conversion to Christ (although I believe that converted Israelites have resettled Palestine as part of the Church, both in a spiritual sense and a physical sense). It would though be more accurate to describe the current State of Israel as the State of Judah, although even that is not the full story as will be discussed in a later chapter.

There are also questions relating to New Testament passages that speak of remaining Jews coming to faith before Christ returns. The promise is that remaining Jews will be grafted into the olive root once again because of God's love for the patriarchs. That is an important promise that should be a matter of love and prayer, but nowhere does it indicate that this must be in a political or nationalistic sense with the formation of a State of Israel. While it is good that some Christian Zionists, such as David Pawson[84], reject Darby's dispensationalism, there

---

[84] Pawson, Op.cit.

is also a need to question why an expansionist, political state is necessary. God's remaining promises to (as yet) unrepentant Jews can be fulfilled without the formation of an identifiable Jewish state. Evangelical Christian theology generally focuses on God's kingdom as being separate from the nation state, which is why many find nationalistic, Christian Zionism out of keeping with the general thrust of Christian teaching. Yes, Christians do seek to shape the state in which they live in a prophetic sense so as to bring it in line with Christian principles, but not in a nationalistic, racial sense where one race is considered to have sole rights over the land. A nation state, like Britain for instance, ideally seeks to bring people of all nationalities together, under one government. Surely, whatever government exists in the Holy Land, and whatever ethnic mix is found there, the Christian approach should be to call for unity and justice between all communities. I think Stephen Sizer does make a valid point in his book that political Zionism has an unnecessary nationalistic edge to it because it favours one people group over and above another, and this isn't something Christians should support.[85]

The State of Israel started out as a simple call for a homeland for Jews where they could live safely, but it may be questioned whether that vision has now been replaced by another vision that is based on military expansionism against its neighbours. An analogy between the conduct of Israel in the Old Testament and the present day is also mistaken, as it is really supporting a return to the judgments of the Mosaic Law that have been rendered obsolete in Christ because he took the punishment for sin upon himself. Today the Law of Moses is summed up in Christ in terms of loving one's neighbour. There is some irony in the fact that those Christians who argue that the State of Israel may legitimately apply Old Testament standards in driving out the Palestinians, do not themselves wish to return to live under the same Law, and neither does the secular

---

[85] See Sizer, (2007) Op. cit

political state in fact abide by the Mosaic Law. Therefore I find it hard to see how the State of Israel is fulfilling a positive prophetic role when Christ's teachings and authority are rejected.

Statement 5 – Help with the ingathering of Jews

'Christian believers are instructed by Scripture to acknowledge the Hebraic roots of their faith and to actively assist and participate in the plan of God for the ingathering of the Jewish People and the Restoration of the nation of Israel in our day.'

Christians cannot help but acknowledge their Jewish roots when Jesus, the disciples, and the first Christians were Jews, and I have tried to do this in this book. This is also exactly what the Church has sought to do by arguing that it is spiritual Israel, although the development of replacement theology by an increasingly Gentile Church led to a gradual loss of recognition of the Church's ethnic Jewish roots. This lack of recognition has been severely criticized by Christian Zionists, and perhaps there is some merit in this criticism. However, it may be acknowledged that replacement theology, as commonly understood, does not provide the full picture of Israel's place in God's plan.

The second part of this statement is more problematic. It is not easy to find a clear Scripture where Christians are instructed to assist the ingathering of Jews into a separate state. It does speak (*Isaiah 49*) that Gentiles will help with such an ingathering of Israelites, but I have argued that this was fulfilled in the Church age where the gospel went out to the twelve tribes in exile, and to Jews and Gentiles, but there is no clear instruction in the New Testament that Christians are to engage in such activity in order to construct a state of Israel populated only by Jews. But there is a clear instruction to preach the gospel of Christ to all people, including Jews, as the great commission of Jesus given to his followers to make disciples of all nations throughout the world.

If it is God's will that a State of Israel should exist at the present time, then God is more than able to bring about such a situation himself without human help and simply permit it, or allow it to happen. In fact it would be hard to imagine that Israel could exist as a state today unless God has at least allowed it. And this I think is one of the strongest cases that can be made for the State of Israel, that God has permitted it to exist for whatever purpose. But questions concerning the purpose of Israel, and how Christians should be involved in its establishment, are separate issues. Pawson argues that God has brought Israel back, and it is his sovereignty that establishes all nation states therefore it logically follows that the establishment of Israel is by God's decree. However, even if we accept this (and it is hard to deny) it doesn't necessarily follow that the State of Israel is living according to God's directive will and purpose today, any more than the nation states of France, Japan, Iran or North Korea are, and these nations too have been allowed to exist according to God's sovereign choice. Applying the commission of Jesus to 'go and make disciples of all nations' implies that Christians should be involved with the State of Israel in a prophetic sense bringing the teachings of Christ into the political arena, and in witnessing to the Jews that Jesus Christ and his perfect sacrifice, are free gifts to Jews according to the fulfillment of the promise given to Abraham. But many Christian Zionists reject the thought that this promise is for all Jews and Israelites, and within Israel any Christian witness or evangelism to Jews is severely restricted by the State of Israel. However, there are Messianic communities in Israel where Jews have accepted Jesus as the Messiah, and they need our support and prayers. Furthermore, the Messianic witness to Jewish people is something that needs Christian support and prayer.

Many Christians though appear confused by the distinction between God's permissive will and his directive will.

God allows many things to happen according to his sovereignty, i.e. his permissive will, and some of these are spoken of in prophecy such as in the book of Revelation. But some of the things that God allows to happen are identified as sin in the Bible. Not that God is encouraging sinfulness, but that he doesn't intervene directly and straight away against every sin that takes place in the world. God's plans are being worked out over time according to a divine plan. However, Christians are not called to participate in helping along that permissive will because that would imply that Christians are called to encourage the growth of sin. Instead Christians are called to live by God's directive will, calling people and nations into obedience in Christ so that sin might be done away with. It is through the Church that God is bringing obedience to his directive will. While for instance Revelation speaks of ungodly things to come, Christians have a commission to fulfill that we are expected to be carrying out faithfully when he returns.

Chapter 9

The Teachings of John Hagee

Pastor John Hagee is one of the foremost Christian supporters of the State of Israel believing God has called the nation to fulfil a divine plan. This is the subject of a recent book *In Defense of Israel*. Hagee is the senior pastor of Cornerstone Church in San Antonio, Texas, which has 19,000 members, and has more recently established a group called Christians United For Israel (CUFI) in America. The stated goals of this group are to build support for Israel in America, and to communicate and educate the pro-Israel perspective to American politicians. Hagee's recent book, *In Defense of Israel* takes his pro-Israel theology a stage further. He also highlights the injustices carried out against the Jews by Christians through history.

Hagee is a controversial figure, and in the past has argued that people and nations must bless Israel in order to be blessed by appropriating the sevenfold blessing given to Abraham (*Gen. 12: 1-3*) to the modern State of Israel. This claim is repeated in this latest book[86] where he comments that those who curse Israel will also be cursed. Seemingly Hagee overlooks Paul's statement that Abraham's blessing has come upon the Gentiles by faith, through Christ's sacrifice (*Gal. 3: 14*), and that through Christ the curse of the Law has been removed because Christ became a curse for all. Instead, Hagee seems to argue that Christians can only partake of the blessing of Abraham *by blessing Israel.* This misappropriation of the blessing in effect encourages Christian compliance to his views through fear. David Pawson follows a similar line of reasoning in his own book, *Defending Christian Zionism*, asking whether we fear the God of Israel.[87] Of course it is right to have a

---

[86] Hagee, *In Defense of Israel*, Zondervan, 2008, pp. 111-119
[87] Pawson, Op. cit., p. 156

respectful and reverent awe towards God, but that doesn't seem to be the point Pawson is making, although it is not clear to whom he is referring when he uses the name Israel. Is he referring to Israel as a state, or Jews as a people group?

Such assertions though invite further comments. The question is really asking whether we have fear towards the State of Israel because the Jewish state is seen as God's chosen agent, but we may legitimately ask who Israel is today? Should we fear the State of Israel, or the Jews, because they still have Abraham's blessing and Christians don't? As we have seen, Paul asserts in his letters (*Gal. 3: 14*) that Christians have been given that blessing of Abraham. Christians, who now have that blessing, should of course love and respect God, and people of all races and nationality including Jews, but not live under an unhealthy fear that is not godly.

Hagee also comments that first century replacement theology was anti-Semitic with the inference being that modern adherents are equally guilty by association.[88] Hagee's description of replacement theology is though a poor characterisation and although such teaching has existed in Church history it does not represent what the New Testament actually teaches. However, use of such inflammatory language and accusations of anti-Semitism against anything that is not liked does not help understanding. To be fair, Hagee does make some valid criticisms of Christian persecution of Jews through history, and those opposed to expansionist and nationalistic political Zionism need to recognise and acknowledge the suffering of Jews, and also to demonstrate love for Jews while rejecting Zionism as an ideology. However, Hagee takes the argument too far by commenting that Hitler's deeds were motivated by his Christianity. As already noted, Hitler in fact believed in a nationalistic 'Positive Christianity;' a faith devoid of any substance and in fact closer to atheism or pantheism. Many Christians were opposed to Hitler's fascism, and paid

---

[88] Hagee, Op. cit., p.145

with their lives, although some acquiesced and stayed within the nationalistic German Church.

But as a result of Hagee's type of pro-Israel teaching some Christians today are finding such appeal in the modern State of Israel that they are turning away from the redemptive sacrifice of Jesus, and looking to re-establish the Old Testament system of worship and rebuild the temple in Jerusalem. In his most recent book Hagee takes another step in this direction by arguing that the old covenant is not dead and by claiming that Jesus did not intend to be the Messiah to the Jews.[89] It would seem that in making such a case Hagee has in fact taken a step away from the traditional gospel message as given in the Bible. In this section of his book he comments that Jesus was not offered as the Messiah to the Jews, and that he was not authorised by God to use supernatural signs to prove he was the Messiah of Israel.[90] Hagee claims that Jesus repeatedly told his disciples to tell no one of the miraculous works that he was doing, thus refusing to even claim to be the Messiah.[91]

According to Hagee, Jesus only intended to be the saviour of the world, and refused to be the Jewish Messiah, commenting that Jesus rejected the role of Messiah in both word and deed.[92] For Hagee, if Jesus were the Jewish Messiah he would have been a conquering ruler who would have sought to gain the support of the general public for the purpose of the overthrowing the might of Rome.[93] But for Hagee, Jesus' comment that 'My kingdom is not of this world' (*John 18: 36*), recorded in John's Gospel, rules him out as the Jewish Messiah. While Hagee rejects Jesus as the Messiah, he is happy to call Jesus 'Christ,' seemingly (and remarkably) unaware that the

---

[89] Hagee, Op. cit., pp. 121-169; 158
[90] Hagee, Op. cit., p. 137
[91] Hagee, Op. cit., pp.139-140
[92] Hagee, Op. cit., p. 143, 145
[93] Hagee, Op. cit., p. 139

word 'Christ' (Anointed One) has exactly the same meaning in Greek as 'Messiah' does in Hebrew.

Hagee appears to use Scripture very selectively taking passages out of their proper context. At one point he makes use of *Matt. 12: 39-40* to build his case, in which Jesus compared the sign of Jonah to his own ministry where the 'Son of Man [will be] three days and three nights in the heart of the earth.'[94] Leaving aside the given sign of the crucifixion and resurrection, Hagee simply makes the point that Jonah went and preached to the Gentiles in Nineveh and that Jesus was simply comparing himself to Jonah's ministry by becoming the saviour and preacher of righteousness to the Gentile world. However, looking at this passage in context shows Jesus condemning the Pharisees as 'an evil and adulterous generation' for seeking a sign, and that the repentant Gentile men of Nineveh will stand in judgement over the unrepentant Pharisees, and their *generation* (*Matt. 12: 38-41*).

In Jesus' prolonged discourses with the Pharisees and Teachers of the Law he concluded by commenting that their house will be left to them desolate (*Matt. 23: 1-38*), then using a Messianic phrase he commented that '…I tell you, you will not see me again until you say, 'Blessed is he who comes in the name of the Lord.' (*Matt. 23: 39*) In Hebrew this statement is *Baruch ha ba be shem adonai*, which is recognised as a greeting by Jews as being Messianic. Jesus was therefore saying to the Pharisees, and Teachers of the Law that he was their Messiah, and as such the only way to find the Messiah was to recognise and accept him.

The apostle John, in his letters, warns against those who downplay the place of Jesus as Christ, calling them deceivers and antichrist (*1 John 2: 22-23*; *2 John 1: 7*) If the State of Israel is being raised to such a level by some Christians that it stands in the place of Christ, and if some Christians are teaching that Jews do not need to come to Christ, then isn't that the type of

---

[94] Hagee, Op. cit., pp. 137-138

deception that John warned against? Those strong supporters of Christian Zionism need to be aware of the dangers and consider whether they are deceiving or being deceived in their excessive love for the State of Israel. It is noteworthy that Pawson in fact rightly criticises this theology of Hagee, and also rejects dispensationalist Zionism.[95]

As discussed in previous chapters, the Old Testament prophecies show the promised ruler was to come through Judah and David, and to be a blessing to all nations. The blessing that Jacob spoke over Judah (*Gen. 49: 8-12*) was that the sceptre would not depart from him, and that a ruler would come who would bring obedience to the nations. Later we find that this ruler was to sit on David's throne establishing righteousness forever (*Isa. 9: 7*) and that his purpose was to bring salvation to Judah as both King and Priest (*Jer. 23: 5-6 & Jer. 33: 15-18*). As noted, in the *Magnificat* (Mary's Song) we find that in Jesus there is help for Israel according to the promise given to Abraham (*Luke 1: 54-55*), and in Zechariah's song also there is joy that Israel is to have a saviour and redeemer from the line of David, according to the promises given to Abraham and the prophets (*Luke 1: 67-79*). In other words Jesus was to be the saviour and promised Messiah to the Jews first, and that his kingdom rule, on the throne of David, would continue forever even extending to the Gentiles. Regrettably Hagee ignores these prophetic words and only refers to Simeon's comments (*Luke 2: 27-32*) that Jesus was to be a *light to the Gentiles*.[96]

For the first few years the early Church mainly consisted of the remnant tribes of Judah, Levi and Benjamin and continued to focus on the Jewish nature of Christianity, only later did more and more Gentiles join. In Orthodox Jewish tradition a person could be considered Jewish through birth, marriage or conversion (although Hagee rejects this traditional Jewish view in favour of belief in Jewish national salvation due

---

[95] Pawson, Op. cit., p. 84-5
[96] Hagee, Op. cit., p. 133

to election alone).[97] The early Christians did not straight away forget their Jewish identity. James, Jesus' half brother, for instance continued to pray in the temple for several decades after the ascension of Jesus, even gaining the name 'camel knees' according to *Eusebius' Ecclesiastical History* (1:XXIII). Jesus was the Messiah to the Jews first, and many accepted him forming the base of the Church, but many Jews did not, and newly converted Gentiles took their place.

However, it is apparent that the apostles were concerned about the degree to which Jewish practices should be followed, as there were those within the Church who favoured a return to the old traditions of Judaism. Later, Paul points out that the old covenant system of worship has passed away for good and has been replaced by the promised new covenant (*Gal 4: 21-31*). He goes so far as to compare the old city of Jerusalem with its temple worship to Hagar because her son was not born of the promise of God. According to Paul, those who continue to follow the old covenant system of worship are in fact in slavery, while the New Jerusalem is above and is free according to God's promise. Therefore, through Christ's perfect sacrificial death, the old covenant system of sacrifice and worship has been superseded and thus rendered redundant.

But when we study prophecy it is a danger to take one or two prophecies out of context without understanding the wider message. When Jesus came to the Holy Land as the Messiah many Jews missed his coming because they were looking for a physical conquering king who would overthrow the Roman Empire, not realising that God was looking for spiritual renewal first. As noted, Hagee seems to be repeating this error in his book, and seems to be arguing that Jews today do not need to come to their Messiah.

Jesus further condemned the Pharisees for their exploitation and brutality (*Matt 23*) and the discourse between Jesus and the Pharisees is of profound political significance. As

---

[97] Hagee, Op. cit., pp. 49-56

such, if we turn a blind eye to the suffering of Palestinians believing that God will bless Israel whatever they do, we are mistaken. While it is of utmost importance to call for the rights of Palestinians to be respected, and Jews too, I do not believe that it is right for Christians to call into question the State of Israel's existence as a political entity, legally established in human terms; that question should be left to God who has allowed Israel to exist according to his permissive will. Political activity should be focussed on being a prayerful, prophetic witness to the Jewish state. Hagee does though make a valid point about the suffering of Jews in history, and Jewish people should be able to see the love of Christ in Christians. However, love for Jews doesn't mean an uncritical support for Israel and its political and military activity. Love towards Jews, as a people, shouldn't now be turned into suffering and hatred for the Palestinians. God's purpose now is not to exclude Palestinians from their own legally established land, as the expansionist policies of the State of Israel appear to be doing. I think that Hagee means well in his love for Jews, but it is a love that is not properly thought through in terms of its impact for both Jews and Palestinians.

Zion's New Name

Chapter 10

Is the State of Israel Jewish?

Another question that ought to be asked is whether the population of the State of Israel today is really Jewish? At face value this may seem like a rather obvious question, but it is not quite as straightforward as many believe. Who are the people who make up the present day State of Israel? Firstly, the Jewish nation in fact had forcibly assimilated the Edomites (descended from Esau, Jacob's brother) in 125 BC. The Edomites had a complex relationship with the Israelites, sometimes showing hostility, sometimes cooperation, but they always desired Jacob's blessing because they believed that Jacob had stolen it from Esau, and therefore they were willing to accept their forced conversion. Esau, as the first born son and heir of Isaac, had in fact sold his inheritance to his younger brother for the price of a bowl of lamb stew, and Jacob had obtained the blessing of his father by pretending to be his more hairy older brother. Esau pleaded with his father for some blessing, but all he received was that one-day he would cast off his younger brother's ascendancy and rule over him for a short time. Later the tribe of Edom came to rule Judea under the half Edomite King, Herod the Great, and at last, at least in part, fulfilled the blessing Isaac had given to Esau for a short period of time (*Gen. 27: 40*). The people of the land of Israel, in the time of Christ and Jews today, are, and were, in part Edomite, although equally they are in part Jewish.

There are a number of other important points relating to research on the people now residing in the State of Israel. A diverse ethnic grouping that appears to form the majority in Israel today are descended from the Caucasian Khazar people of central Asia, a people who converted to Judaism some time around the late eighth century or early ninth century AD. One Jewish historian, Arthur Koestler, has called these non-Semitic

Jews, the Thirteenth Tribe.[98] The Khazar kingdom was positioned between the Christian centres of power in Europe and the growing power of Islam that was extending northwards. Not wishing to join with either the Christians or the Muslims they sent for Pharisees and Rabbis to come to their land in order to teach them the ways of Talmudic Judaism.

Khazar descent is believed to be through Kozar a son of Togarmah, and as a nation they once formed part of the Gokturk Empire. For this reason some opponents of the State of Israel have suggested that the majority of the Israeli populace are in fact related in some way to Gog and Magog, which would put a different twist on the prophecy of *Ezek. 38-39*. However, it is not possible to establish this claim authoritatively without further research and information, as there could be a number of possible candidates for Gog and Magog including Turkish and Islamic forces that have invaded and ruled in Palestine in the period since the New Testament times, or perhaps it represents an invasion from the north that is yet to come. God in fact slowly reveals the meaning of prophecy in the proper time, and the real identity of Gog and Magog will I believe also be revealed one day according to God's timeframe.

But what happened to the Khazar Jews? Although there is some disagreement, the general idea is that the Khazars spread to Poland when their empire collapsed and later became identified as Ashkenazi Jews. It is possible that there were already Jews living in Eastern Europe at this time and that these people later assimilated with the emigrating Khazar Jews through intermarriage. The fact that the Ashkenazi or Khazar Jews are largely Caucasian and not Semitic doesn't necessarily mean that the people of Israel today should not be identifiable as ethnically Jewish. The most ethnically distinct Semitic Jews today are Shepardi Jews who traditionally remained around the Mediterranean Sea coasts, but often found themselves expelled

---

[98] Koestler, A., *The Thirteenth Tribe*, Random House, 1976; See also; Brook, K.A. *The Jews of Khazaria*, Rowman & Littlefield Publ. 2006

from their settled cities from time to time. As noted in the previous chapter intermarriage with foreigners doesn't stop a community remaining a legitimate expression of Judah. What does seem to hinder being a legitimate expression of Judah-Israel is faith, and outside of Christ the Jews cannot receive the promise of God because Christ was the fulfilment of the promise given to Abraham.

Another point to consider is the origin of the six pointed, Star of David, Shield of David or Magen David on the Israeli flag (and displayed prominently on the cover of Hagee's book *In Defense of Israel*) that is also of interest. Although a beloved symbol of many Christian Zionists, it cannot easily be traced to Old Testament Judaism and it would seem that instead it was a Babylonian or Persian astrological symbol or amulet known as the 'King's Star' that became associated with Israel through occasional infiltration of pagan and Babylonian idolatry. However, in the interest of fairness, if anyone has compelling evidence to the contrary I would be interested in hearing it. But for this reason, some Orthodox Torah Jews refuse to use it as a Jewish symbol believing it to be occult. Furthermore, a group called *True Torah Jews Against Zionism* argue that the State of Israel does not represent the Torah faith of Moses, or the real Jewish people, and are opposed to Zionism because they believe the modern State of Israel has not been sanctioned by God and accompanied by repentance, but is the work of man through Talmudic Judaism.

The Talmud is a vast collection of writing that includes the Mishnah, which is a standardised form of the largely oral Pharisaic Tradition of the Elders. In the time of Jesus the Mishnah existed amongst the Pharisees and was passed down from father to son (*Matt. 15: 2*). Jesus in fact condemned this tradition because the Scribes and Pharisees were using it to nullify the Law of Moses for their own selfish ends. While the Torah Jews today hope for a full restoration of a Jewish state they believe repentance must come first according to the Mosaic Law (*Deut. 4: 29-31*). It was the prophecy of Jeremiah that caused Daniel to repent on behalf of the Jewish people that then led God to heal and restore the Jews to the Promised Land at the end of their Babylonian exile (*Jer. 29; Dan. 9*). For this reason Torah Jews believe the State of Israel is illegitimate without repentance coming first.

But the question remains regarding the Jewish identity of the modern day Israeli population. Ethnically, the resident people of Israel are at least in part Jewish under the traditional understanding of what it means to be Jewish, but spiritually most are still living outside of God's promise to Abraham, a promise that can only be received through faith in the Messiah who was the true seed of Abraham. However, there are Jews in Israel who have found faith in Jesus as their Messiah, and they need the support and prayers of Christians as they seek to bring their kinsfolk back into fellowship with God's one olive root, that is only to be found in Jesus.

Chapter 11

What promises remain for Jews?

While I believe that a straightforward reading of many of the Old Testament prophecies relating to Israel are being fulfilled in the Christian Church (that is, I believe, spiritually, legally and ethnically a union of Judah and Israel together with Gentile believers) Jesus said that the fig tree, representing unrepentant Judah, would again appear bearing green leaves, but not fruit. This is, I believe, what we see today in the State of Israel, a state identifiable as ethnically Jewish in part, but in many ways secular and rejecting the teachings of Christ and nullifying the writing of Moses. Instead there is a continued interest in the Talmudic interpretation of the Mosaic Law that developed out of the Tradition of the Elders. The State of Israel shows outward glory, but does not see the necessity for bringing forth the fruit of the Spirit that Jesus desired and required.

But that is clearly not the end of the matter. Paul wrote in the letter to the Romans that in the end all Israel will be saved because of the promise of God to Abraham. This is to happen once the full measure of the Gentiles has been brought into the Kingdom of God. Paul further exclaims; '...how much greater riches will their fullness bring!' and comments that if 'they do not persist in unbelief, they will be grafted in again' (*Rom. 11: 23*). According to Paul 'Israel has experienced a hardening in part until the full number of the Gentiles has come in. And so all Israel will be saved...(*Rom. 11: 25-26*). ' Paul also noted that '...they are loved on account of the Patriarchs... (*Rom. 11:28*)' and, '...they too...may now receive mercy as a result of God's mercy...' (*Rom. 11: 31*).

In the present time it is to be hoped that this promise is not far off from being fulfilled. Christians should support the work of evangelism to the Jews taking place in Israel under very difficult circumstances and urge the Jewish authorities to remove legal restrictions. Such laws are preventing Jews from receiving the promise of God given through their forefather Abraham, and fulfilled through Christ. Some Christian Zionists are also hindering Jewish people from receiving the full promises of God by suggesting that they can still approach God through the Mosaic legal sacrifices, and urging Christians not to witness to, or evangelise Jews in Israel, or elsewhere. However, the perfect, loving sacrifice that Jesus made upon the cross is for all Jews and Gentiles, given according to God's own promise. With similar sentiments, the North American grouping of the Lausanne Consultation on Jewish Evangelism recently issued a statement on the importance of evangelism to Jews following its 26th annual meeting (2-4 March 2009) in Pheonix, Arizona. The statement rejects dual covenant theology and reasserts that the gospel is for Jews, both in the land of Israel and elsewhere, even as a priority, commenting further that to deny the gospel to Jews is not a loving response and is detrimental to their best interests.

Abraham received a seven-fold blessing that is for all Israel and this covenant is greater than the Law of Moses, both to Jews and Gentiles, according to their faith. Genesis (*Gen. 12: 1-3*) records this blessing, but note that the blessing is not just for Abraham and his direct descendents, but that all people on earth will be blessed through him. The fruit that God requires is that the blessing is shared and passed on.

> 'I will make you into a great nation, and I will bless you.
> I will make your name great, and you will be a blessing.
> I will bless those who bless you, and who ever curses you I will curse;
> and all peoples on earth will be blessed through you.'
> (*Gen 12: 2-3*)

Paul, in the letters to the Romans, Galatians and Ephesians, notes that this blessing has passed to the Gentiles through Christ, but that in the end all Israel will partake in the blessing because of what Christ has done, and because of God's own promise. In the end the once rejected remnant of Jewish people will receive grace to believe in Christ. There is only one rootstock as a channel of grace and God's desire is to bring Jews and Gentiles together in that united olive tree, which is today the Christian-Messianic community of believers.

One fear though today that many are concerned about is that Israel is in danger from its Islamic neighbours. Neither does modern Israel appear to rely on the grace of God for its defence, but believes that its own power and strength can save it from harm with help from a powerful and wealthy America. Israel is multiplying its armaments in contradiction of God's command to trust him, also forgetting that Jacob was given his new name of Israel because of the necessity for reliance upon God for blessing and protection, unlike the younger Jacob who tried to fix his own blessing. It would though be a great tragedy if the State of Israel suffered major loss before the Jews in Palestine receive their promised blessing in Abraham through Christ. There is great danger for the people in the State of Israel today who live outside of Christ.

There are many people from around the world who have hoped and prayed for the conversion of Jews in Israel, but that has not happened yet to any great extent, even after sixty years of nationhood, and there is much resistance to evangelism in both Israeli society and in legislation. God, in his mercy, has so far protected Israel from serious harm, but that mercy is so that the Jews in Israel might turn to him. The Israelis cannot resist God's grace forever through rebellion and reliance on their human strength without suffering the consequences, as their own biblical history attests to so clearly.

Tony Pearce, like Hagee, and many other supporters of the State of Israel, applies the blessing of Abraham to the modern State of Israel, and develops the theology of the pre-tribulation rapture in his book *The Omega Files*,[99] but unlike some of the more extreme Christian Zionist teachers, he

---

[99] Pearce, Op. cit.

recognises the problem of unbelief in Israel today. For Pearce, Israel will sign a false peace treaty with the antichrist in order to escape destruction at the hands of the global enemy. However, they will be betrayed and suffer major loss. According to Pearce, it will be out of that suffering that the Jews of the world will finally accept Jesus as the Messiah. This, according to Pearce, will then herald in the final part of the second coming of Christ.[100]

While I do not necessarily agree with this scenario, it is of interest in order to highlight the fact that many Christian Zionists do not think through the eschatological consequences of what is being taught, but simply have placed their hope and trust in the visible State of Israel as evidence of God's activity in the world, instead of placing their hope and trust in the presently invisible Messiah. It is almost as if Israel, as a visible state, has replaced the Messiah in the minds of many Christians. There is danger in this I believe, not least because Christians run the risk of being deceived by false teaching. Christianity in the West is already under attack from many sides; the new atheists are writing and selling books by the million, and the faith of other Christians has grown faint with a deistic spirit having replaced the dynamic faith of the first century Christians. As a result of the activity of militant atheism that is undermining people's faith, new age or neo-pagan groups seem to be attracting many supporters with their post-modern beliefs and ideas, and the concept of truth itself is being lost.[101] Christians are also being wearied by economic crises and war in the Middle East where the supporters of political Zionism are fighting the forces of militant Islam. There has been recent war in Iraq, and continuing conflict in Afghanistan, and talk in the press at this time concerning America and the West engaging in war with Iran to

---

[100] Pearce, Op. cit., p. 79.

[101] The meaning of 'truth' in atheism is merely illusionary, because atheism ultimately destroys the notion of meaning and logic. The atheists have no consistently logical and objective way of establishing their claims.

prevent that Islamic state obtaining nuclear warheads. Pakistan is also unstable with its dangerous nuclear weapons at risk of falling into the hands of the Taliban. A war with Iran would be for the stated purpose of protecting Israel from a possible future nuclear strike, but there are great risks in such an endeavour apart from the serious ethical problems.

As well as the obvious concern about this scenario, a second concern then is that if Islamic forces were to succeed in destroying the State of Israel then it could prove a fatal blow to the faith of many Christians, this because those Christians have placed such high hopes and faith in Israel believing the nation is fulfilling a divine plan, and not really understanding the complete theology of Christian Zionism and what it entails.

Islam too is greatly feared in the western world, although I think such fears are over exaggerated. The strength of the Church has always been in humble service, love and forgiveness, while building goodwill for Christ amongst the people of the world. Islam instead lacks the ability to generate sufficient goodwill and unity needed for world domination. For these reasons, I do not believe that Islam can ever spread across the world by force of arms because it does not create that goodwill, but only a grudging and hateful compliance to brutal dictatorial rulers. By seeking to conquer by force, the Islamic people lose their God given humanity not recognising that truth cannot be imposed by force of arms. The truth of God can only be received by revelation from God. But equally the western world and Israel cannot defeat Islam by force, but only by showing the love of Christ to Muslims while engaging in respectful dialogue, thus preaching by deeds not only by words. This was the mistake of the Crusades; Christians only empowered Islam by seeking to impose their Christian will on them by force and the western nations are making the same mistake today (although in reality the West is so secular these days that it would be more accurate to say that it is secularism that is seeking to impose its will on Islam by force at the present time).

Whatever happens to the State of Israel in the future, there will still be more Jews living outside of Palestine and the gospel will continue to go out to them until Christ returns, and right up to the end they will continue to be offered grace to believe in Christ. The land of Palestine was always too small to contain the full promise given to Abraham, and God's purpose was to bless the whole world through his people by scattering them around the world and then bringing them to faith in Jesus Christ. The descendents of Abraham, especially through Joseph and Ephraim, were to become very numerous upon the earth. This is the promise of God to Israel today, but it is being fulfilled through Christ and the Church community. Jesus said to his disciples 'I tell you the truth, you will not finish going through the cities of Israel [preaching the gospel] before the Son of Man comes [returns]' (*Matt. 10: 23*). The promise to Jews today is the promise of restoration in Christ and the offer of being re-grafted back into their own natural olive tree; this by returning to Christ in obedience to God.

But how should we consider the status of the Jewish nation today before God? Has God abandoned the state completely and replaced it with the Church, or does God really have two groups of people on the earth under a dual covenant? If we consider the teachings of Hosea that were spoken against the Assyrian exiles, and apply them to the present day Jews, then it may be seen that the unrepentant nation is in effect being unfaithful towards God by rejecting Christ. And, just as God divorced the northern tribes of Israel for their pagan idolatry, God too has legally divorced the present day segment of Jews who rejected Christ (*Hos. 2: 2-7 & Matt. 23*). However, just as God sent the northern tribes of Israel away, he continued to remember and love them. In the same way, God also remembers and loves the present day Jews, just as Paul said in Romans, but the current status of unrepentant Judah is that of a divorced woman. Still loved on account of the Patriarchs, but presently legally separated. The only way for the Jewish people to be reunited with God's true community of believers is through acceptance of Christ's work upon the cross (*Rom. 11: 31*). In that way Jews may be remarried to God under the new covenant, there can be no way back to God through the old one.

As for seeking to understand God's plan for the present day State of Israel, I believe it is possible that God has brought Jewish people into the land so that he can pour out his Spirit upon the people in the nation and thus lead them to genuine spiritual revival, and also to a lasting and just peace settlement with the Palestinians; where Muslims also need to come to Christ. Without wishing to limit God's purposes in the world it should be acknowledged that it is possible that God desires that Jews live in the land under the new covenant. A Christian vision for God's people in the Holy Land then should be one where Jews are to be re-grafted into their natural olive tree and thus become united with Palestinian Christians and other Gentile believers. The Christian-Messianic community in Palestine is, I believe, the true Israel in the land, not the secular and nationalistic political State of Israel. I believe that this should be the focus of Christian' support for Israel, and of those who feel called to love and work amongst Jews; that is a vision of peace, justice and reconciliation in Christ. It needs to be remembered that there is the great commission of Christ, that is to bring all nations under his governing authority, and that includes the nations and people of Israel and Palestine.

Zion's New Name

Chapter 12

Conclusions

This has only been a short study, but a number of points can be made. I do not believe that replacement theology as generally characterised, or the theology of modern Christian Zionism, provide accurate theological frameworks regarding the place of Israel today, whether as a spiritual entity or as a state in God's scheme of things in the present time. Although there is in fact a wide spectrum of thought, and categorising individual opinion is difficult. However, from this study the following points can be identified and stated.

Point 1. What is often a hindrance to understanding the status of true Israel is an incomplete grasp of Old Testament history and the prophetic writings. While Abraham's blessing is known (and often misapplied), Joseph, Ephraim and Manasseh's possession of Israel's birthright is often missed, as is the northern exile of Israel in 721BC by the Assyrians. This exile meant that the birthright was removed out of the land, with the Israelites then scattered across the earth as Jacob-Israel promised to Joseph's sons, especially Ephraim. God's plan, through Abraham and his descendents, was to bless the whole world. Biblical prophecy continued to speak about the northern tribes of Israel in exile, and the promise of *their* spiritual restoration was even spoken of in the later period of the prophet Zechariah. Many supporters of Christian Zionism ignore the fate of the northern tribes of Israel, believing them to be replaced and rejected for good, and then misapply prophecies that relate to the scattered northern Israelites to the establishment of the modern State of Israel by the descendents of Judah. However, Judah did not possess the birthright, instead the Judaic tribe had the wonderful promise to bring forth the ruling Messiah.

Point 2. Furthermore, because strong supporters of Christian Zionism, such as Hagee, are seemingly downplaying the place of Christ and suggesting that Jews do not need to come to Christ, which is perhaps an extreme form of Darby's erroneous dispensationalism, then it may be asked whether another gospel is being preached. Supporters of Christian Zionism need to be aware that this development is bound to invite another serious question; is the formation of the State of Israel really part of God's plan, or is it part of a deception that the apostle John warned against?

Point 3. I believe that a correct understanding of Scripture shows that the Christian Church is in a very real sense spiritual Israel because of the promises given to Abraham that are now to be received by faith. Israel then continues as the Christian Church today, not as having replaced Israel, but as true Israel, where Jews, Israelites and Gentile believers dwell together, united in the one olive tree. As Paul notes, the true Israelites are those who have faith in Christ because of the promise given to Abraham, and Abraham was the man of faith whose trust in God was accredited to him as righteousness. So the Church is fulfilling and continuing the covenant of promise given, by God's own name, to Abraham, and under the promised Judaic-Davidic ruler, Jesus the Messiah. This covenant of promise cannot be replaced and is greater than the mediated covenant of Moses that has been rendered obsolete. What has been replaced then, by Christ's perfect sacrifice as the Lamb of God upon the cross, is the sacrificial requirement of the Mosaic Law whereby the blood of animals was necessary to take away the sins of the Jews and Israelites on an annual basis. Now Christians are to live by the spirit of the Law, which is love. That part of the Mosaic Law was only ever meant to be an interim measure to lead people to Christ when the time had come for Christ to be revealed. Christ came in fulfilment of the greater promise given to Abraham that has not been replaced, but continues in the Church and is received by faith, and this worldwide Church of Jesus Christ is now spiritual Israel and the Kingdom of Heaven upon the earth where this new Israel is being built up together as God's perfect tabernacle in Christ's own body.

Point 4. The Christian Church is also ethnically related to both Judah and Israel. The first Christians were Jews, and many of the early converts were also from the exiled northern tribes of Israel who were dispersed among the nations, and Jesus sent his disciples to them and to scattered Jews during his ministry, and for the first few years after his ascension. It was only after Peter's vision to take the gospel to the household of the Gentile Cornelius, (where God says he has made the repentant Gentiles 'clean') and Paul's calling to preach to the Gentiles, that the Church's ministry was extended to Gentiles. This may be seen as a fulfilment of Old Testament prophecies relating to the reunification of Israel and Judah, (and there are a number of them that form a consistent pattern as has been shown from Jeremiah, Isaiah, Hosea, Zechariah and Ezekiel etc), together with an ingathering of many Gentiles into the initially Jewish Church. Later this Israel, that is the Christian Church, resettled Palestine and established communities in the land as a literal fulfilment of prophecy, but the real Kingdom of God that Jesus spoke of in his parables was a spiritual kingdom that would grow and extend across the earth, as for instance a mustard tree grows across the whole garden, but also where the wheat and the weeds would grow up together (*Matt. 13*). In other words, although Jews and Israelites joined the Church at its instigation, they were resettled into God's kingdom as spiritual Israel; a body of believers that was growing across the world and extending to Gentiles, and not just resettled as a small ethnic group into a single nation in a small piece of land in the Middle East.

Point 5. As noted, the Christian Church, as spiritual Israel, did resettle Palestine following the overthrow of the Jewish nation by the Romans in AD 68-70 in a literal fulfilment of prophecy. The true Israel, as well as spreading across the world, today maintains continuity in the Holy Land from the first century AD. It also follows from this that the present day

Palestinian Christian community continues this lineage and needs the support of other Christians. Encouragingly, some Messianic Jewish believers have been grafted back into their natural olive root also.

Point 6. The Christian Church is also legally Israel in terms of the covenant of Abraham because Jesus, through the apostles he sent out, shepherded the flock of the house of Israel. In doing this he reunited the Israelite northern tribes that included Ephraim and Joseph (who were scattered, but possessed the birthright), with the remnant of Judah (who brought forth the Messianic Sceptre), together with the in grafted Gentiles. In other words, the legal birthright that Jacob-Israel possessed from Isaac and Abraham, and passed on to Joseph and Ephraim, is now in the Christian Church because Jesus brought the remnant of Joseph and Ephraim under his governing authority according to scriptural prophecy. The first disciples also formed a legally established Jewish community with 120 men according to Jewish customs. I want to emphasise though that while these legal and ethnic arguments are important, the spiritual aspect is of greater importance.

When we come to the present day status of the State of Israel and the Church there are a number of further points that need to be considered.

Point 7. God clearly has allowed a Jewish State of Israel to arise and exist within the last one hundred years, although the reasons for this are not entirely clear. While this state legally exists in human terms, and seems to have been given an opportunity to fulfil some form of divine purpose today because God has allowed it to exist, God's purposes are often difficult to understand until they are revealed in full. Today there is only a partial revelation regarding the identity of the State of Israel. I believe that some of the teachings of Christian Zionism overlook the general thrust of God's purposes revealed through biblical prophecy and fulfilled in Christ and the Church. New Testament Pauline theology cannot be used to suggest that there will be a return to the old covenant system of worship, because Jesus has abolished that system for good by his perfect sacrifice.

According to the Gospels, Judaism cannot now bear the fruit that God requires without the Messiah, even though Jesus said that the fig tree of Israel would again appear sprouting more green leaves, but not fruit. According to the Mosaic Law the Jewish restoration to the land of Israel was to be accompanied first by repentance. Trying to establish the State of Israel apart from repentance and outside of Christ is in effect disobedience towards God. In other words, although God has permitted Israel to exist as a secular state for whatever reason, the state is not actually living in obedience to God's directive will and purpose. I do not believe that God can ultimately bless such a situation.

The idea that the State of Israel can exist as part of God's kingdom outside of the Christian Church goes against the clear teaching of Scripture, which teaches unity with one olive root on which all the branches of Israel and Judah must eventually be grafted. I do not believe that the State of Israel, as a nationalistic Zionist state, can fulfil a divine purpose today outside of Christ, and I question how Christians can rightly support nationalistic expansionism in the land against the Palestinians. However, this study has no interest in opposing the existence of the modern State of Israel as a political entity, I will leave that up to God if there is any opposing to be done, but neither do I believe that Christians should support the State of Israel in that nationalistic sense. A Christian's first calling is to Christ and his spiritual kingdom, upholding it in love, justice and righteousness, and in this regard Christians and Messianic believers should provide a prophetic voice to the State of Israel, calling the state to obedience under the Messiah. It is important to love the unrepentant Jewish people as they, like all of us, are in need of salvation in Christ.

Point 8. The status of the two-third's part of the Jewish nation that rejected Christ, and therefore is not at present included in the Messiah, is akin to that of a legally divorced woman. They are therefore still loved by God on account of their forefathers, but not at present legally his people. God's desire is that Jews return to him and accept Jesus and thus be reunited with the true Israelite olive tree.

Point 9. There are many Palestinian Christians and Messianic Jews in Israel today seeking to witness to the Jews, and they need our support and prayers. Christians are indeed called to love Jews, as Christian Zionists such as Hagee rightly note, but sadly some do not accept the Messianic witness to Jews. However, some biblical prophecies (such as *Rom. 9-11*, and also *Zech. 12: 10*) point to the final conversion of Jews to the Messiah in the last days and this should be a matter of encouragement and prayer. Jesus also asserted (*Matt. 10: 23*) that the gospel message must, and will continue to be preached to the Jews and Israelites until he returns. This is because of God's promise to Abraham, and Paul notes in Romans that the unrepentant Jews *now* are loved on account of the Patriarchs and will therefore receive grace to believe *now*, and up until the end. Equally, the Palestinians who are Christian need our love, support and prayers as they seek to live in difficult conditions. We cannot overlook their suffering either and as Christians we should seek to work for peace and justice in the land between both communities.

As noted, it is possible that God desires a Messianic community of ethnic Jewish believers in the land before Christ returns, but once again the Christian community should not be divided between Jews and Gentiles, between Jewish believers and Palestinian Christians. In fact those Israeli citizens who do accept Christ join with the true Israel of God in Palestine, and an expansionist and nationalistic State of Israel is wholly unnecessary for God's purposes to be competed.

I believe then that Jews need to accept Jesus as their Messiah in order to fulfil their purpose in God's plan; anything else would imply that God has two kingdoms under a dual covenant, but such theology divides Israel from the Messiah along neo-Platonic or Gnostic lines. But as Paul noted there is only one kingdom, one olive rootstock on to which both the

Jews and Gentiles are to be grafted. It is also important to recognise that the Palestinian Christian community can be traced back to the earliest Christian believers, an ethic mix of Jews and Gentiles. This lineage I believe represents the true Israeli occupation of the Holy Land in a literal sense; but also in a spiritual and legal sense as well as the ethnic one, as a continual resident people in the land according to God's promises, and also as part of the worldwide Christian community. Furthermore, it is legitimate to ask questions about the treatment of Palestinians, especially as it relates to the indigenous Christian community in Palestine.

It is being argued here then that the relationship between the Christian Church and historical Israel is one of unity and continuity where the Church is spiritually, ethnically and legally Israel, thus forming the true olive tree that is being built up together in Christ's body. God has indeed made a promise to Israel that cannot be broken and is being fulfilled in the Christian Church. The full promise to Israel though may be considered to be as part of the continual conversion of Jews to the Messiah, an ongoing process that is not yet complete. Christ's work on the cross was in fulfilment of the promise given to Abraham, but Paul notes that in the end all Israel will be saved, suggesting that the full measure of unrepentant Jews and Israelites will one day be united in accepting Christ, alongside the wider Christian community. This is, I believe, the remaining promise of God to all Israel, to Jews and Israelites inside and outside of the Middle East, and should be the focus of Christian love and concern for Jews.

A Vision for the State of Israel

Ideally, I would suggest that a Christian vision for governance of the Holy Land should be one that seeks to bring Israel, Gaza and the West Bank together, perhaps with a joint state with a confederate structure, where there is greater unity between Jews and Palestinians, both communities united, working and living together in Christ. What is needed is spiritual expansion in Christ, not an expansion of the possession of land. Christians should further pray for the government in the State of Israel that it develops policies that are in line with Judeo-Christian truths and values. Such values follow the principles of the Law of Moses that have been interpreted by Jesus Christ in terms of love being the fulfilment of the Law. Christians should not oppose the right of the Israeli state to exist, such rights are given and taken away by God, and Christians are called to have a servant spirit, but with a prayerful, prophetic edge. In the same way, although the Old Testament prophets pronounced God's will to the Israelite rulers, they never opposed the nation in their own name. The same principle I believe applies to all states, whether secular western nations or predominantly Muslim nations as well. Those people and nations who oppose God's loving righteousness and justice will be brought to a place where they must account for their action and learn obedience through God's discipline. Interestingly, there are Jews in Israel who too seek peace and justice for Palestinians in the land. The *Israeli Committee Against House Demolitions* has as its main goals justice and a sustainable peace settlement for both sides, which allows for 'security, dignity and freedom' together with economic development, perhaps under a regional confederation of states.[102]

Whether the Jewish people inside the State of Israel take advantage of the opportunity to fulfil a divine purpose by receiving Jesus Christ as the Messiah and following his path of righteousness remains to be seen. Whatever happens to the State of Israel in the future, and there is concern over that question, there will remain an opportunity for Jews resident and living inside and outside of the State of Israel to receive their full promises, given to Judah and Israel, in Jesus Christ until He returns.

---

[102] [http://www.icahd.org/eng/about.asp?menu=2&submenu=1]

Zion's New Name

Appendix 1 - Jerusalem Declaration on Christian Zionism

Statement by the Patriarch and Local Heads of Churches In Jerusalem 22nd August 2006

"Blessed are the peacemakers for they shall be called the children of God." (*Matt. 5: 9*)

Christian Zionism is a modern theological and political movement that embraces the most extreme ideological positions of Zionism, thereby becoming detrimental to a just peace within Palestine and Israel. The Christian Zionist programme provides a worldview where the Gospel is identified with the ideology of empire, colonialism and militarism. In its extreme form, it places an emphasis on apocalyptic events leading to the end of history rather than living Christ's love and justice today.

We categorically reject Christian Zionist doctrines as false teaching that corrupts the biblical message of love, justice and reconciliation.

We further reject the contemporary alliance of Christian Zionist leaders and organizations with elements in the governments of Israel and the United States that are presently imposing their unilateral pre-emptive borders and domination over Palestine.

This inevitably leads to unending cycles of violence that undermine the security of all peoples of the Middle East and the rest of the world.

We reject the teachings of Christian Zionism that facilitate and support these policies as they advance racial exclusivity and perpetual war rather than the gospel of universal love, redemption and reconciliation taught by Jesus Christ. Rather than condemn the world to the doom of Armageddon we call upon everyone to liberate themselves from the ideologies of

141

militarism and occupation. Instead, let them pursue the healing of the nations!

We call upon Christians in Churches on every continent to pray for the Palestinian and Israeli people, both of whom are suffering as victims of occupation and militarism. These discriminative actions are turning Palestine into impoverished ghettos surrounded by exclusive Israeli settlements. The establishment of the illegal settlements and the construction of the Separation Wall on confiscated Palestinian land undermines the viability of a Palestinian state as well as peace and security in the entire region.

We call upon all Churches that remain silent, to break their silence and speak for reconciliation with justice in the Holy Land.

Therefore, we commit ourselves to the following principles as an alternative way:

We affirm that all people are created in the image of God. In turn they are called to honour the dignity of every human being and to respect their inalienable rights.

We affirm that Israelis and Palestinians are capable of living together within peace, justice and security.

We affirm that Palestinians are one people, both Muslim and Christian. We reject all attempts to subvert and fragment their unity.

We call upon all people to reject the narrow world-view of Christian Zionism and other ideologies that privilege one people at the expense of others.

We are committed to non-violent resistance as the most effective means to end the illegal occupation in order to attain a just and lasting peace.

Zion's New Name

With urgency we warn that Christian Zionism and its alliances are justifying colonization, apartheid and empire building.

God demands that justice be done. No enduring peace, security or reconciliation is possible without the foundation of justice. The demands of justice will not disappear. The struggle for justice must be pursued diligently and persistently but non-violently.

"What does the Lord require of you, to act justly, to love mercy, and to walk humbly with your God." (*Mic. 6: 8*)

This is where we take our stand. We stand for justice. We can do no other. Justice alone guarantees a peace that will lead to reconciliation with a life of security and prosperity for all the peoples of our Land. By standing on the side of justice, we open ourselves to the work of peace - and working for peace makes us children of God.

"God was reconciling the world to himself in Christ, not counting men's sins against them. And he has committed to us the message of reconciliation." (*2 Cor. 5: 19*)

Authors:

His Beattitude Patriarch Michel Sabbah - Latin Patriarchate, Jerusalem. Archbishop Swerios Malki Mourad, Syrian Orthodox Patriarchate, Jerusalem. Bishop Riah Abu El-Assal, Episcopal Church of Jerusalem and the Middle East. Bishop Munib Younan, Evangelical Lutheran Church in Jordan and the Holy Land.

Appendix 2 - Christian Presence in Palestine

The Christian community residing in Palestine today covers various denominations and is known as *Nasrani* (from Nazareth) or *Masihi* (from Messiah) and they have always had great respect for the land, which they identify as the Holy Land. The earliest Christians were present in the land in the first few centuries of the Christian era, later flourishing with the conversion of the Roman Empire to Christianity during and following the time of Constantine. Although many of these Christians were Jewish converts, a large number of Gentiles and undoubtedly some Israelites from the Diaspora joined with them from various nations.

The Maronites, centred now in Lebanon, are followers of the fourth century Syrian monk St Maron, and formed an independent Christian community speaking Aramaic; later they accepted Roman Catholic authority, but maintaining a degree of independence. From the fourth century to the Islamic influx and conquest in the seventh century, Jerusalem was a prosperous centre of the Christian community in the land, although the Christian community did not seek to rebuild the temple as they were instead looking for the New Jerusalem. A Christian presence has remained in the land through various periods of crusades and Muslim rule, and during times of peace the community has flourished and even by the time of the Ottoman Empire the numbers remained relatively high. At the end of the nineteenth century under the Ottoman rule, 30 percent of the inhabitants in Palestine were thought to be Christian. However, the number of Christians in the land has fallen dramatically in the past 100 years.

By the time of the British Mandate rule in Palestine the number of Christians were of the order of 18 to 20 percent having fallen steadily from the Ottoman period, but remained fairly constant from 1922 to 1947.[103] Wagner reports that according to a British census the number of Palestinian Christians in Jerusalem in 1922 was around 51 percent of the population. Most were from the well-educated mercantile class. However, following the UN partition of 28th November 1947 between 725,000 and 775,000 Palestinians, including many Christians, were expelled. Wagner quotes the historian Sami Hadawi, who estimated that over 50 percent of Christians in West Jerusalem were expelled, which represented the largest reduction in Christian numbers in Palestinian history. More Jerusalem Christians were expelled than Muslims following the land grab of 1948-1949 with 37 percent of Jerusalem Christians becoming refugees. This disparity was because Christians were concentrated more in the western part of the city that was seized by Israel. Of the land seized by Israeli authorities some 34 percent had previously been owned by Palestinian Christian churches with no compensation given.[104] Between 1947 and 1950 both Christian and Muslim Palestinians were expelled throughout the Israeli controlled areas. According to the Israel State's own statistics there were only 35,000 Christians remaining in the Jewish controlled area in 1950, representing some 3 percent of the total population. Seemingly, hundreds of thousands of Christians had been forced out. By 1995 the number of Christians in the State of Israel had increased to 160,000 people, but little change in percentage terms.[105]

Sociologist Bernard Sabella of Bethlehem University reported that in the Palestinian controlled areas of the West Bank, East Jerusalem and Gaza the number of Christians had

---

[103] Wagner, D., "Palestinian Christians: An Historic Community at Risk?" *Information Brief,* No. 89, 12th March 2002; and Charles M. Sennot (2007) *The Body and the Blood: The Middle East's Vanishing Christians and the Possibility for Peace.* Public Affairs, 22

[104] Wagner, Op. cit.

[105] Population by Religion and Population Group, Israeli Central Bureau of Statistics, 2004 [http://www1.cbs.gov.il/shnaton56/st02_01.pdf] Accessed Sept. 2008

declined from 18 percent in 1947, to 13 percent in 1966, and a massive fall to only 2.1 percent by 1993, and 1.6 percent by 2002. This fall is attributed to the Israeli military occupation by Wagner, and to a lack of security and economic and social stability in Palestinian areas caused by Muslim terrorism, which has led to continuous emigration out of the land by the Christian people.[106]

---

[106] Wagner, Op. cit.

Appendix 3 - Israel in the Old Testament Prophets (table)

	1. Israel to be restored to the land under the Messiah	2. Israel and Judah to be reunited under the Messiah	3. The kingdom extending to the Gentile nations	4. The restoration of Israel under a New Covenant
Amos	Amos 9: 11-12		Amos 9: 11-12	
Hosea	Hos. 3: 4-5	Hos. 1: 10-11	Hos 2: 21-23	Hos. 2: 14-20
Isaiah	Isa. 1: 12-16; 49: 5	Isa. 11: 10-12	Isa. 14: 1-2; 49: 6; 49:19-20; 56:3-8; 65:1-2	Isa. 49: 8
Micah	Mic. 2:12-13; 5:2-4		Mic. 5:4-5	
Jeremiah	Jer. 23: 5-6; 30: 8-10; 33: 17	Jer. 23:5-6; 30:1-4; 31:27; 31:31-34; 50:4-6		Jer. 31:31
Ezekiel	Ezek. 34: 11-24; 37:24-28	Ezek. 37: 15-23		Ezek. 34: 25-31 Ezek. 37: 24-28
Zechariah	Zech. 10: 1-5	Zech. 8: 13; 10: 6-12	Zech. 9: 11-14	Zech. 9: 11-13

This table is a summary of central themes relating to Israel in the Old Testament prophets as discussed throughout this book. What is shown consistently in the Old Testament prophets is that the promises of God included restoration of the northern tribes of Israel to God, together with reunification with Judah and union with the Gentiles. All of this was to take place under the new covenant that God was going to make with his people.

Although there was the promise to Israel that they would repossess the land, the land was considered too small to contain the large number of Israel's offspring because they had spread across the earth and multiplied, fulfilling the promises of God, which were to bless Abraham, Isaac, Jacob, Joseph and Ephraim with abundant fruit. Therefore, through Christ, God extended the borders of Israel to include all the earth, but within the new Kingdom of God.

Appendix 4 - The Lost Tribes of Israel

It has been noted that there are similarities between some European names, and names relating to the tribes of Israel. Denmark, as a name, is suggested to be close to the tribe of Dan, Iberia, Ireland and Hibernia perhaps sound like 'Hebrew' and the Saxons and Scots could be identified as the Beth Sacae, or the house of Isaac, while others have claimed that the Celtic name Cymru (pronounced Cumri) relates to the house of the Israelite king Omri.[107] Further lines of evidence for this claim come from the discovery and translation of the Behistun Inscription, a multilingual inscription on Mount Behistun, which was written in antiquity before 400BC, and still exists along the ancient road from Babylon to Media. Henry Rawlinson translated the large text between 1835 and 1843, and it consists of the same statement in three languages, Old Persian, Babylonia and Elamite. The Old Persian and Elamite texts identify the Sacae, Saka or Scythian people with the Gimirri, or Cimmerian on the Babylonian part of the text. Furthermore, the Assyrians who conquered the northern tribes of Israel identified the people of Israel as the House of Khumri, named after Omri the notable King of Israel in the 8th century BC.[108] George Rawlinson commented that he thought he had;

'...reasonable grounds for regarding the Gimirri, or Cimmerians, who first appeared on the confines of Assyria and Media in the seventh century B.C., and the Sacae of the Behistun Rock, nearly two centuries later,

---

[107] These claims were made in the late 19th century by Sir John Rhys, *Early Celtic Britain*, pp. 142, 150 & 162-3

[108] For instance Capt. Raymond, E., *Missing Links Discovered in Assyrian Tablets* Artisan Pub, 1985

as identical with the Beth-Khumree of Samaria, or the Ten Tribes of the House of Israel.'[109]

However, while this may be of interest to some it really would require a thorough investigation of the evidence to establish authoritatively and is therefore beyond the scope of this present study. I also find these ideas too British or European centric, when in truth the exiled Israelites were scattered across the world, as far as India and China as well as Europe.[110] For these reason it is not the intention here to make such a link and thus I will leave aside the question of whether a link exists in reality. But, bearing in mind the fact that according to Scripture the Israelites were scattered across the earth, and Jesus' comments relating to the work of preaching to the scattered Israelites throughout the world (*Matt. 10: 23*), such a link would be entirely consistent with scriptural teaching (See also for instance the promise to Ephraim (*Gen. 48: 15-16*)).

So what happened to the lost tribes of Israel? A plain sense reading of Scripture suggests that many were subsumed into the emerging Christian Church, (a process that is not yet complete) and then gradually lost their separate Israelite identity. But it means that the Church is in part ethnically Israel (as well as having ethnic links with the first Jewish Christian believers). Some Christians may argue that this is quite a tenuous argument, but I would point them to study the words of the prophets in the context of the political and historical setting in which they wrote, as I have tried to do in this book. Furthermore, it also needs to be remembered that what is important to God is not ethnic identity, but spiritual identity in Christ, where the Church is being built up together as spiritual Zion with people from every ethnic group.

---

[109] Rawlinson, G., Taken from a note in his translation of *History of Herodotus*, Book VII, p. 378

[110] In the 1920s Thomas Torrance for instance tried to identify the Chiang-Min people of West Szechuan Province in China as Israelite exiles.

Appendix 5 - Questionable Documents

There are a number of works that are worth mentioning that are of questionable origin and of a conspiratorial nature. The purpose of this is to shed some light on what are controversial, but for some, rather appealing documents. The first is the Protocols of the Elders of Zion. This work has long been considered a forgery, although sometimes those who object to their authenticity seem to protest a little too much. Whatever their origin, I doubt that they are truly of Jewish origin; perhaps instead they are the work of the Nazi fascist propaganda machine. There is no point in discussing the Protocols in further depth because they are of dubious origin and therefore a red herring and not central to the message of this book. Furthermore, discussing them tends to generate more heat than light.

Another aspect for consideration is holocaust denial that is increasingly common today. At times some have sought to downplay the holocaust suggesting that six million Jews did not really die in the Second World War. In response, I would comment that there is no real reason to deny that millions of Jews suffered and died in the war, and there is no real reason to deny a figure of six million as a reasonable rounded estimate of numbers who died. Quite clearly many Jews have suffered greatly through history, and this needs to be acknowledged and remembered. Also, it needs to be recognised that undoubtedly millions of people died in the war from many other nations, as well as those who identified themselves as Jewish.

The third work of interest is the letter from Albert Pike, a leading freemason, to the mafia boss Giuseppe Mazzini, dated to 15th August 1871 and involving a blueprint for three world wars.[111] The stated aim of this letter was to bring about the final

---

[111] Anyone wanting a reference can easily find the letter through an Internet search.

destruction of Christianity and institute a religion of Lucifer in its place. However, the authenticity of the letter has not been established convincingly.

The letter was first mentioned by Cardinal Caro y Rodriguez of Santiago, Chile, in his book *The Mystery of Freemasonry Unveiled* in 1925. Rodriguez mentions in that year that the letter was in the possession of the British Museum. However, William Guy Carr, a former Intelligence Officer in the Royal Canadian Navy, obtained a statement from the British Museum asserting that they did not possess such a letter. Carr writes in a footnote to his 1959 book *Satan, Prince of this World*, that the Keeper of Manuscripts informed him that this letter is not catalogued in the British Museum Library, therefore its origin must be in doubt. The Pike to Mazzini letter was first publicly discussed in 1925, after the First World War, but before the Second.

The letter comments that the purpose of the First World War was to overthrow the Russian Czars, and then build up atheistic communism in that land. Christianity would be weakened through the spread of communism. The Second World War was to be fought so as to strengthen political Zionism sufficiently to allow the formation of a sovereign state of Israel in Palestine. International Communism would be strengthened to balance the power of Christendom.

It may be noted that the Second World War did indeed allow the creation of a Zionist State of Israel in 1948, partly because of a wave of sympathy for the Jewish people as a result of the holocaust. Communism was also strengthened when in 1945 the Potsdam Conference between Truman, Churchill and Stalin handed over a large part of Eastern Europe to Russian control. According to the letter, these developments enabled plans for a third global war. Following the 9/11 events and the subsequent war on terror events could be seen to be moving towards greater conflict in the Middle East. The letter in reality highlights the threats and dangers faced by the people of Israel, and also by Muslims and Christians, if the letter is an accurate reflection of what is happening today.

The letter states that the Third World War is to be fought by exploiting differences between political Zionism and the Islamic World, to the point where they 'mutually destroy each other.' The other nations would be forced to take sides and therefore lead to 'physical, moral, spiritual and economical exhaustion.' Christianity, with its increasingly weak deistic spirit, will be unable to withstand the new atheists and nihilists.

Today, the State of Israel is at times waging war against its Islamic neighbours, who are slowly gaining in organisation and strength, and now increasingly threaten the existence of Israel as a state. With so many Arab and Palestinian Muslims hardened by war, there seems little for them to lose, and they are increasingly turning to desperate measures. In response the State of Israel seems to be fighting back with greater force.

While the letter is of questionable original, there are people, ironically even some Christian supporters of Israel, who seem to be interested in driving events in a similar direction where it is believed that the State of Israel has been established in order to be eventually destroyed through another holocaust. The Islamic world and its culture too is being destroyed and degraded by war and violence. I believe that Christian supporters of Israel need to be aware and concerned that support for political Zionism with its expansionist vision against the Palestinians is in effect playing into the hands of those who seek to destroy the Jewish people and Christianity. Whether the letter has a measure of authenticity and is attributable to the stated author, (which is in doubt) events seem to be playing out in that vague direction anyway. If that is a reasonable proposition, then it may be seen that Israel is in great danger, as well as the Arab nations.

Also, the faith of many Christians who have placed a lot of trust in the State of Israel, believing it is fulfilling a divine purpose in this time, could be shaken. Can it possibly be that the emergence of an expansionist state in Israel is part of a deliberate plan of Satan to provoke war in the Middle East and ultimately destroy the Jewish people and Christian faith? There is no definitive answer to this question at this time and the letter is of questionable origin, but it is something to be aware of. From this I would urge readers not to get too attached to particular eschatological schemes, especially those that involve a separate State of Israel, and a pre-tribulation rapture, because it may endanger their faith when the time of trail comes. The other message from this is that in light of such dangers there is surely a greater onus upon Christians to work for peace and justice in the Middle East between both the Jewish and Palestinian communities in order to bring about a lasting and sustainable peace settlement. Christians need to have a vision for the Holy Land that involves bringing the Jewish people and Palestinians together in Christ, and thus seek to avoid an apocalyptical catastrophe that is possibly being planned by some. Of course God is ultimately sovereign over the states of the world and events that unfold, but Christians have a clear mandate in terms of going throughout the earth and making disciples of all nations seeking to bring all into God's kingdom.

Zion's New Name

Selected Bibliography

Carroll, J., (2001) *Constantine's Sword: The Church and the Jews*, Boston: Houghton Mifflin

Carter, J, (2006) *Palestine: Peace not Apartheid*, New York, Simon and Schuster

Cohen, J. (1991) (ed.), *Essential Papers on Judaism and Christianity in Conflict: From Late Antiquity to the Reformation*, New York: New York University Press

Cruse, C.F. (1995) (trans.), *The Ecclesiastical History of Eusebius Pamphilus - Bishop of Caesarea, In Palestine*, 1850. Reprinted as *Eusebius' Ecclesiastical History*, Baker Book House

Hagee, J., (2008) *In Defense of Israel*, Zondervan

Hood, J.Y. B., (1995) *Aquinas and the Jews*, Philadelphia: University of Pennsylvania Press

Jacobs, J, (1925) 'Tribes, Lost Ten,' in Singer, I., and Adler, C (ed.) *Jewish Encyclopaedia*, Vol.12, New York: Funk and Wagnalls

Jones, S.E., (2002), *The Struggle for the Birthright*, God's Kingdom Ministries, USA

Josephus, (1987) *Antiquities of the Jews, The Works of Josephus,* (Trans.) Whiston, Hendrickson Publishers

Lindsey, H. (1974) *The Late Great Planet Earth*, Zondervan

Novak, D., (2004) 'The Covenant in Rabbinic Thought,' in Korn, E.B. (ed.), *Two Faiths, One Covenant?: Jewish and Christian Identity in the Presence of the Other*, Rowman & Littlefield

Pawson, D. (2008). *Defending Christian Zionism*, Terra Nova Publ.

Pearce, T., (2002) *The Omega Files*, New Wine Press

Robertson, O.P., (2000) *The Israel of God*, P & R Publ.

Rowdon, H. (1967) *The Origins of the Brethren*, Pickering and Inglis

Sennot, C.M. (2007) *The Body and the Blood: The Middle East's Vanishing Christians and the Possibility for Peace*, Public Affairs, 22

Sizer, S., (2004) *Christian Zionism: Road map to Armageddon?* Nottingham: IVP

Sizer, S., (2007) *Zion's Christian Soldiers?* Nottingham: IVP

Soulen, R.K., (1996).*The God of Israel and Christian Theology*, Minneapolis: Fortress

Steer, R. (1997) *George Muller*, Christian Focus Publications

Torrance, D.W., & Taylor, G., (2007) *Israel God's Servant*, London: Paternoster Press

Wagner, D., (2002) "Palestinian Christians: An Historic Community at Risk?" *Information Brief,* No. 89, 12th March

Walker, A, (1985) *Restoring the Kingdom*, London: Hodder and Stoughton

Wilkinson, P.R. (2007) *For Zion's Sake, Christian Zionism and the Role of John Nelson Darby*, London: Paternoster

Wolvoord J.F. and Wolvoord J.E. (1974) *Armageddon: Oil and the Middle East Crisis,* Zondervan Press

Scripture References

Bethesda, (Brethren
assembly), 44
Black Sea, 73
Bonhoeffer, Dietrich, 18
Brethren, 43, 44
Exclusive Brethren, 43,
45
Open Brethren, 43, 44, 45
Plymouth Brethren, 29,
35
British Consulate in
Jerusalem, 29
British Mandate, 13, 144
cabalism, 34
Calvin, John, 26, 27, 39, 42
Calvin's covenant
theology, 26, 28, 39,
41
Cappadocia, 74
Carter, Jimmy, 11
Caspian Sea, 73
Catholic Apostolic Church,
29, 38
Catholic, Roman, 21, 22,
26, 36, 93, 144
Clement (first century), 97
Confessing Church, 1, 18
Constantine, Roman
Emperor, 21, 26, 144
Cornelius, 14, 135
Council of Nicea, 21
covenant
dual covenant, 91, 138
dualistic theology (See
also dualism), 91

covenant theology. *See*
Calvin's covenant
theology
Craik, Henry, 44
Crusades, 129
Cuninghame, 31
Cyprian of Carthage, 20
Daniel, 69, 124
Darby, J.N., 10, 28, 29, 31,
35, 36, 37, 38, 39, 40, 41,
42, 43, 44, 156
David, 25, 35, 54, 57, 69,
76, 79, 81, 83, 87, 117
David's covenant, 27
house of David, 69, 80
Messianic reference, 52,
56, 62, 63, 64, 66, 67,
72, 77, 82
Dead Sea, 67
Diaspora, 75, 144
Gk. diaspora, 76
Gk. diasporas, 75
dispensationalism, 10, 28,
29, 34, 37, 38, 39, 44
Church of Scotland, 29
donkey, 84
foal, 68
Drummond, Henry, 29, 33,
34, 38, 39
dualism, 39, 41, 53
Edom. *See* Esau
Ekklesia, (referring to the
people of God in the Old
and New Testament),, 27
election, 91
Elijah, 90

Ephesians, 96–97
Ephraim, 51, 57, 63, 67, 68
Esau, 90, 121
eschatology, 9, 30, 31, 39,
  43, 46, 47, 48, 128
Esdras. *See* Ezra
Euphrates, 74
Eusebius, 86, 97, 118, 155
Ezekiel, 46, 47, 61, 65, 66,
  67, 135, 147
Ezra, 74
fascism, 114, 151
fig tree, 82, 86, 108, 125,
  137
  green leaves, 87
Frey, Joseph, 30
Galatians, 46, 92, 93, 97,
  103, 126
Gamaliel, 85
Gaza, 13, 17, 145
Gentiles, 32, 39, 42, 43, 46,
  47, 54, 58, 59, 60, 72, 76,
  77, 80, 83, 89, 90, 91, 92,
  93, 94, 97, 101, 104, 107,
  110, 113, 116, 117, 125,
  126, 135, 144, 147
Gnosticism, 49
  Gnostic teachings, 41
Gog and Magog, 47, 67,
  122
Gomer, (Hosea's wife), 55
grace, 26, 27, 39, 42, 45, 68,
  69, 90, 91, 92, 93, 95, 96,
  104, 127, 130, 138
Graves, Richard, 36
Groves, Anthony Norris, 35

Hagar, 95, 118
  slavery, 118
Hagee, John, 1, 15, 50, 117,
  113–19, 123, 133, 138
Hebrew, (language), 116
Hebrews, 46, 64, 67, 97, 98,
  99, 100, 101, 103
Herod the Great, 79, 121
Herzl, Theodor, 46
Hitler, Adolph, 18, 114
holocaust, 41, 42, 47, 151,
  153
Holy Land, 60, 105, 118,
  142, 143, 144
Holy Spirit, 13, 33, 38, 49,
  70, 76
Hosea, 55, 56, 60, 61, 90,
  107, 135, 147
Iran, 128
Irving, Edward, 31, 32, 33,
  34, 38, 39
Isaac, 27, 39, 49, 95, 97,
  101, 103, 121, 149
Isaiah, 32, 46, 47, 56, 57,
  60, 61, 77, 107, 110, 135,
  147
Ishtar, 13
Islam, 13, 47, 122, 128, 129,
  153
  Allah, 13
  Islamic, 47, 127
  Islamic conquests, 14
Israel
  Eretz Israel, 50, 106
  house of Israel, 65, 66,
  73, 76

kingdom of God, 80, 125
kingdom of heaven, 80
national calling, 40, 41
northern tribes of Israel,
61, 71
spiritual Israel, 9, 19, 20,
25, 110, 134, 135
State of Israel, 9, 10, 11,
12, 14, 17, 29, 32, 37,
46, 47, 51, 87, 101,
106, 108, 111, 113,
115, 119, 121, 122,
123, 125, 127, 128,
130, 133, 136, 137,
140, 145, 152, 153
Jacob, 27, 49, 57, 58, 59,
60, 63, 67, 79, 90, 101,
103, 108, 117, 121
James, brother of the Lord,
21, 76, 118
Jeremiah, 24, 61, 62, 63, 64,
100, 107, 123, 135, 147
Jerusalem, 31, 34, 39, 48,
49, 61, 67, 68, 69, 70, 73,
75, 76, 82, 84, 86, 93, 95,
101, 103, 105, 115, 118,
141, 143, 144, 145
Christian Patriarchs and
leaders of, 48
Council of Jerusalem, 76
New Jerusalem, 69, 95,
102, 105, 118, 144
Jesus Christ, 12, 13, 15, 27,
49, 72, 93, 94, 97, 98,
111, 130, 134, 140, 141
sceptre of Judah, 103

Jews, 10, 13, 15, 16, 19, 20,
22, 26, 27, 29, 37, 40, 43,
45, 47, 51, 72, 73, 74, 84,
87, 89, 90, 91, 93, 94, 96,
97, 98, 99, 101, 104, 108,
111, 113–24, 125, 126,
127, 130, 134, 155
Jesus' disciples, 53
Messianic Jews, 138
remnant of Jews, 55
Jezreel (God scatters (sows)
the Israelites), 55
Joel, 76
John the Apostle, 67, 84, 85,
115
John the Baptist, 80
John, Apostle, 116
Jonah, 116
Joseph, 51, 57, 67, 68, 79,
80, 108
birthright of Joseph, 25,
40, 104, 133, 136
Josephus, 73, 74, 155
Judah, 25, 51, 52, 53, 54,
55, 57, 58, 60, 61, 62, 63,
64, 65, 66, 68, 69, 70, 71,
72, 73, 75, 79, 82, 83, 86,
87, 100, 103, 107, 108,
117, 123, 125, 135, 140,
147
Judaism, 9, 10, 19, 21, 26,
34, 49, 93, 97, 98, 118,
121, 123, 137, 155
Judeo-Christian, 25
Justin Martyr, 19, 23
Kerala, southern India, 75

Shield of David, 123
Stephen, martyr, 21
Syria, 65
tabernacle, 39, 99, 100, 101
Talmud, 16, 21, 123
temple, 21, 39, 80, 83, 144
  third temple, 41
Tertullian, 20, 98
The Morning Watch, 33, 34, 38
Third International
  Christian Zionist
  Congress, 49, 103
Thomas, Apostle, 75
Timothy, 97
Torah, 16, 85, 123
Tradition of the Elders, 16, 123, 125
Tregelles, Samuel, 44
Way, Lewis, 30
West Bank, 17, 145
Westminster Confession, 26, 28
Wilkinson, Paul, 26, 35, 36
Wolff, Joseph, 34

Zechariah, 61, 68, 69, 70, 76, 79, 80, 82, 83, 91, 117, 135, 147
Zionism
  Christian Zionism, 9, 10, 17, 22, 24, 27, 45, 47, 48, 49, 50, 53, 129, 133, 136, 141, 142, 143, 156
  Christian Zionists, 12, 15, 17, 26, 41, 46, 53, 57, 69, 71, 87, 89, 91, 101, 105, 110, 111, 123, 126, 128, 138, 153
  Christians United For Israel (CUFI), 113
  classic Zionism, 42
  First Zionist Congress (1897), 46
  political Zionism, 10, 37, 46, 128, 152
  Protocols of the Elders of Zion, 151
  Zion, 59, 60, 61, 62, 63, 70, 81, 82, 101
  Zion's new name, 60

Also by Andrew Sibley, *Restoring the Ethics of Creation*

Published 2006 by Anno Mundi Books, P.O. Box 752, Camberley, England, GU17 OXJ. Paperback, 5.5 x 8.5", 316 pp. ISBN 13: 978-0-9543922-2-2 / ISBN 10: 0-9543922-2-1

This book argues that as a result of the rise of the Darwinian faith system and belief in the certainty of technological progress and unrestrained capitalism, we have lost a proper respect for nature and humanity. Ethical standards are now based on subjective criteria where each person is able to decide his or her own conduct, often living for self in a grand struggle for survival. No more is seen the providential God who offers blessing and grace to mankind, nor the divine Sovereign who requires people to live in partnership with his will and purpose.

However, the Christian tradition known as Natural Theology has seen in nature the appearance of design, but more than that, it has pointed to the power, wisdom and goodness of the Designer and goes on to inform our conduct as Paul noted in Romans 1:20. When properly formulated, this twin book approach enriches our lives, with the book of Scripture in the one hand, and the book of nature in the other, giving mankind rights, duties and a purpose in caring for one another and for creation.

If as Christians we are really concerned with ethical standards, then we need to restore and develop a proper understanding of the Natural Theology tradition, both in terms of the appearance of design seen in nature, and also in terms of our response to the Creator. This book also addresses the problem of suffering and brokenness in nature and considers the question of the place of miracles in creation.

Printed in the United Kingdom by
Lightning Source UK Ltd., Milton Keynes
139647UK00001B/59/P